BBQ PIT BOYS

Book of
Real *Guuud*

BARBECUE

MIX
Paper | Supporting
responsible forestry
FSC® C016245

A Firefly Book

Published by Firefly Books Ltd. 2024
Copyright © 2024 Moseley Road Inc.

First printing

Library of Congress Control Number: 2023949666

Library and Archives Canada Cataloguing in Publication
Title: Book of real guuud barbecue / BBQ Pit Boys.
Other titles: Book of real good barbecue
Names: BBQ Pit Boys, author.
Identifiers: Canadiana 20240292758 | ISBN 9780228105114
    (softcover)
Subjects: LCSH: Barbecuing. | LCGFT: Cookbooks.
Classification: LCC TX840.B3 B66 2024 | DDC 641.7/6—dc23

Published in the United States by	Published in Canada by
Firefly Books (U.S.) Inc.	Firefly Books Ltd.
P.O. Box 1338, Ellicott Station	50 Staples Avenue, Unit 1
Buffalo, New York 14205	Richmond Hill, Ontario L4B 0A7

Conceived, designed & produced by Moseley Road Inc.
President: Sean Moore
Design: Adam Moore, Tina Vaughan
Editor: Finn Moore
Cover Design: Philippa Baile, Karen Prince
info@moseleyroad.com

Printed in Canada

Disclaimer
The recipes in this book have been carefully tested by the authors. For those people with food or other allergies, or who have special food requirements or health issues, please read the suggested contents of each recipe carefully and determine whether or not they may create a problem for you. In the event of any doubt, please contact your medical adviser prior to the use of any recipes. All recipes are used at the risk of the consumer.

We cannot be responsible for any hazards, loss or damage that may occur as a result of any recipe use.

For safe consumption, please ensure that all foods described here are cooked to a safe internal temperature:

♦ 165°F (73.9°C) for poultry (including ground poultry)
♦ 160°F (71.1°C) for ground meats and eggs
♦ 145°F (62.8°C) for beef, pork, veal, lamb steaks, fish and shellfish

These temperatures are the safe *minimum* internal temperatures for these meat and meat products according to the USDA. For reasons of personal preference, consumers may choose to cook their food to higher temperatures.

Book of
Real *Guuud*
BARBECUE

CONTENTS

INTRODUCTION   8

CHAPTER 1

BURGERS & SAUSAGES

Mushroom & Onion Hamburgers   18

Hell Burger Bacon Cheeseburger   20

Double Cheese Bacon-Bang Burgers   22

Bacon Cheeseburger Deluxe   24

Beer Can Bacon Burger   26

Steak 'n' Bacon Cheeseburger   28

Bacon Veggie Burgers   30

Whiskey Bacon & Egg Cheeseburgers   32

Potato Chip Bacon Burgers   34

Reaper Ghost Cheeseburger   36

Beef Bacon Liver Burgers   37

Jalapeño Bacon Chuck Burgers   38

Bacon Pig Dogs in a Blanket   40

Grilled Sausage 'n' Peppers Sub   42

BBQ Sausage Sandwich   44

Grilled Kielbasa Sausage   46

Bison Sausage & Kraut Sandwich   48

Peppered Pork Bacon Butter Burger   50

CHAPTER 2

MEATLOAF, MEATBALLS & PIES

Meatloaf Hamburger Supreme   54

BBQ Meatballs   56

Pepperoni Pizza Pie   58

Grilled Beef Pot Pie   60

Cheese & Bacon Meatball Sub   62

Guinness Meatballs   64

Cajun Jambalaya   66

BBQ Bacon Meatball Stuffed Onion   68

Beef 'n' Bacon Mozzarella Balls   70

Fireball Whiskey Meatballs   72

CHAPTER 3

BEEF

Steak 'n' Bacon Scallop Sub   76

Steak & Oysters Seafood   78

Lobster-stuffed Filet Mignon Steak   80

Rib Steaks & Scallops with Clam Sauce   82

Tri-Tip Steaks   84

Strip Steak & Whiskey Gravy   86

Rib Steaks & Bacon Potato Bombs   88

Beef Rib Roast   90

London Broil Grilled Steak   92

Top Sirloin Beef Roast   94

Beef 'n' Whiskey Kebabs   96

Teriyaki Beef Tenderloin   98

Oxtail Beef 'n' Beer Stew   100

CHAPTER 4

OTHER MEATS: PORK, LAMB & GAME

Butterscotch Bourbon Ribs	104
Margarita Ribs	106
Asian Grilled BBQ Ribs	108
St. Louis Spare Ribs	110
Grilled Bacon Ribbits	112
Pit Boys Pork & Beans	113
Whiskey Glazed Smoked Ham	114
Stuffed Pulled Pork	116
Apple Butter Tenderloin	118
Leg of Lamb	120
Rack of Lamb	122
Spit Roast Leg of Lamb	124
Grilled Lamb Chops	126
Venison Stew	128
Braised Rabbit with Olives	130
Alligator Tenderloin	132
Mushroom Ragout with Venison	134
Stuffed Alligator BBQ	136

CHAPTER 5

POULTRY

Competition Chicken Thighs	140
Smoked Turkey Wings	142
Pound Chicken	144
Grilled Chipotle Chicken	146
Chicken Wing Loaf	148
Nacho Wings	150
Buffalo Wings Grilled Chicken Style	152
Chicken Dragon Eggs	154
Chicken Pig Cheese Wraps	155
Hot Wing Kebabs	156
Chicken Cheese Thighs	158
Apple Cider Smoked Turkey	160
Wild Goose Breast	162
Cornish Game Hens	164
Grilled Pheasant	166
Coconut Chicken Drumsticks	168
Smoked Boneless Turkey Breast	170
Thai Stick Chicken Wings	172
Turkey with Stuffing & Wild Turkey Gravy	174
Chili Chicken Sub	176

CHAPTER 6

FISH & SEAFOOD

Stuffed Clams	180
Salmon with Ginger Chili Sauce	182
Pale Ale Mussels	184
Drunken Clams & Shrimp	186
Fried Crawfish Po'boy Sandwich	188
Crab Cakes	190
Pepper Shrimp Kebabs	192
Crispy Fried Fish & Chips	194
Pepperoni Clams & Mussels	196
Butter Smoked Scallops on the Grill	198
Grilled Fish with Corn Salsa	200
Pistachio Crusted Grilled Fish	201
Black Iron Pan Fish	202
Pirates Fish Stew	204

CONTENTS CONTINUED

CHAPTER 7

SOUPS, SALADS & SIDES

Smoke Grilled Onion Soup	208
Bacon Chili Corn Chowder	209
Bacon Cheeseburger Soup	210
Bacon & Cheddar Potato Soup	210
Grilled Potato Salad	212
Pineapple, Chicken & Avocado Tomato Salad	213
Black Bean Salad	213
Mac & Cheese	214
Black Iron Potatoes	215
Candied Bacon Jalapeño Smoked Cream Cheese	216
Chipotle Shrimp Stuffed Peppers	217
Grilled Jalapeño Poppers	218
Strawberry Bacon Jalapeño Poppers	219
Sweet Bacon Cornbread	220
Stuffed Cabbage in Hot Chili Sauce	221
Bacon Stuffing	222
Bread Stuffing	222
Lobster & Brandy Stuffing	222
Fire-roasted Chili Pepper Relish	223
Grilled Corn Salsa	223

CHAPTER 8

SAUCES, GRAVIES, RUBS & MARINADES

Liquid Gold BBQ Sauce	226
Vodka BBQ Sauce	226
Alabama White Sauce	227
Clam Sauce	227
Orange Ginger BBQ Sauce	228
Chili Beer BBQ Sauce	228
Independence Day Hell Fire Hot Sauce	229
Bourbon BBQ Sauce	230
Jalapeño Beer BBQ Sauce	230
BBQ Sauce Country Style	231
Jalapeño Honey BBQ Sauce	231
Baby Sweet Coke BBQ Sauce	232
Mint Sauce	232
Kansas City BBQ Sauce	233
Cigar Ash BBQ Sauce	233
Meat Gravy	234
Steak & Bourbon Gravy	234
Onion Gravy	235
Bacon & Scallion Crème Gravy	235
Country Style Rib Rub	236
Mud Rub	236
Coffee Dry Rub	237
Kansas City Dry Rub	237
Chili Rub	237
Homemade SPG	238
Classic American Rub	238
Dry Rub for Ribs	238
Pepper Rub	239
Cajun Dry Rub	239
Tender & Moist Pork Marinade	240
Beef Jerky Marinade	240
Margarita Marinade	241
Chairman Goose Marinade	241
Orange Chili Chicken Marinade	242
Beer & Chili Marinade	242
Marinade for Steak	243
Asian Marinade	243

CHAPTER 9

DESSERTS

Cinnamon Whiskey Pumpkin Pie	246
Blackberry Rhubarb Pie	248
Chocolate Banana Dessert	250
Grandma's Grilled Apple Pie	251
Cherry Chocolate Pie	252
Irish Cream Cherry Pie	253
Grilled Bacon Bourbon Crème Brûlée	254
Bacon Oreo BBQ Cookies	255

CREDITS & ACKNOWLEDGMENTS	256

OPPOSITE main: Jeff Goldblum joins the Pit Boys for a cookout, filming for an episode of his Disney+ show, *The World According to Jeff Goldblum.*
top left: Jesse, Bob's son, who is managing the BBQ Pit Boys
top right: Bob, with his grandson, Chase.
bottom left: Bob with family.
bottom right: The pit!

INTRODUCTION

Founded in the US in 2007 as a YouTube cooking channel, "BBQ Pit Boys" is now a worldwide fraternal order, with more than 18,000 Chapters and 230,000 Pitmasters in over 100 countries. The Pitmasters starring in the show are known for publishing videos of "old-time" grilling methods, as well as new recipe inventions and innovative techniques, using mainly meat products (and a fair amount of booze!). Since its debut, the channel has released an episode every Sunday, and their videos have been viewed almost 1.5 billion times. It is hosted by Bobby Fame and a group of his friends, and as he explains—it started almost by accident...

I've always loved cooking outdoors—it's what I grew up with. By trade I was an antiques dealer, and when YouTube first started I thought it might be useful for my business. When my son, Jesse, got married, I bought a video camera (thinking a video of the wedding would be a great present), but my real motive was to make videos for my new online antiques business! Around the same time I came across an old kettle grill at our local dump. I took it home and I cooked up some dishes with my buddy, Jack, who was visiting at the time from California. Some time later Jack called for advice about cooking the dish—so I thought the simplest way would be to cook it again while filming it and send Jack the video.

I finally managed to upload it to YouTube for Jack to see. I was real surprised to get a call from YouTube suggesting the idea of partnering with them. And a month after that a check arrived for 32 bucks! People were watching the video I had made for Jack—and I was receiving payment for it!

So that was that! We were having fun doing something we loved and being paid for it—what's not to like?! We made more videos and cooked more dishes. I have no professional background in food whatsoever. I learned about the fire as a cub scout and I have become a bit better by learning from lots of mistakes, often having no idea what I'm doing.

"This is more than just a cookbook, it's a way of life!"

Bobby Fame

We experiment & we have fun!

With over 5 million subscribers across social media and more than 1,000 instructional videos, the BBQ Pit Boys have spread all over the world—even as far away as Tokyo and New Zealand!

And, as crazy as it sounds, we are proudly ranked in the top 5% of all YouTube channels and we are the #1 BBQ channel! Our videos are the real deal; we take pride in producing realistic, clear instructions on how to get the best results when grilling, minus all the hot air and frills typical to food shows.

We like to present the whole outdoor grilling and barbeque experience—to share the fun, camaraderie and creativity we have at the grill with our viewers—to demonstrate that anybody can in fact do this, and that they can also have the same experience that we have. We're just guys hanging out, grilling and shooting videos, with a side of comedy, intentional or not!

INDIRECT HEAT

DIRECT HEAT

TECHNIQUES

Our videos and recipes explain the tools you'll need and the cooking methods you'll use, like how and when to use the "low & slow," and the values of "direct" or "indirect" heating. Low & slow is probably obvious, of course—it simply means to cook the meat at a lower temperature for a longer period of time—but we also advise which cuts of meat and joints each method is appropriate for.

"Indirect" and "direct" cooking refers to how the grill is set up. We generally set the grill up with hot coals on one side, and no coals on the opposite side. With direct cooking, the meat is placed directly over the hot coals for high heat and searing. With indirect cooking, the meat is placed on the opposite side of the grill, away from the coals, so it will bake or roast more gently.

THE MOTHER PIT

We have built up the Pit (the Mother Pit, as we affectionately call her) over the period of time we've been cooking and grilling, so since 2007. We now have about 20 grills that we use regularly. We often have visitors, friends, or family who bring a contribution, and we share the experience of grilling together.

We're just guys hanging out, grilling & shooting videos.

We appeal to the everyday griller, who loves to be outside but might be intimidated by the process.

SPG SEASONING—AND MORE

Here at the Pit, we've come up with some personalized blends of rubs, sauces, and seasonings that we put on just about everything. One of our all-time favorites is SPG seasoning, or salt, pepper, and garlic. It's simple, effective, and it works with almost anything that goes on the grill.

If you like the sound of that, you can pick up some BBQ Pit Boys seasonings yourself—or, as always, you can make or use any kind of seasoning you like. We encourage you to experiment and adapt our recipes by using your favorite spices, rubs, and sauces—we advise how and when in the videos. You can take the bare bones of the recipes and experiment as you like, or you can follow our recipes exactly. If you want to make your own SPG seasoning at home, all you need to do is mix equal parts salt, pepper, and garlic, and apply it liberally to your favorite cuts of meat before they go on the grill.

Kick-back good eating around the Pit doesn't get any better than this!

THE BBQ PITBOY CODE

Our ethos is simple—it's about being authentic and true to our beliefs: good quality, good humor, good company. We approach grilling in a straightforward way, to make it satisfying and fun—and so take the stress out of it! We are avid fishermen and hunters, real environmentalists, and teach a sustainable harvest.

We don't follow rules; we're Family Grillers, not BBQ purists. Our philosophy resonates globally, celebrating the relaxed lifestyle at the heart of the American dream.

We're about more than just just cooking and eating, we're about teaching and sharing the skills to grill confidently. Our community values camaraderie, offering support and advice among members, and bringing generations together, from fathers and sons, mothers and daughters, to lifelong friends.

We are the antithesis of typical over-produced network food TV. At the Pit, it's all about the meat, the fire, and the primal joy of cooking outdoors.

It's about showing the ease and simplicity of having a go at grilling and BBQ.

It's about the beards.

It's jeans and work boots, not fashion.

It's cheap beer, bourbon, and cigars.

It's a lifestyle.

It's global.

It's BPB4L—"BBQ Pit Boys For Life!"

Bobby Fame

"The BBQ Pit Boys are the embodiment of the American dream of a relaxed lifestyle, which has been enthusiastically taken up by our fans around the world."

BURGERS & SAUSAGES

SAVOR THE IRRESISTIBLE FLAVORS OF JUICY MEAT COOKED PIT BOY STYLE. SICK OF THOSE PLAIN OLD GRILLED HAMBURGERS? TRY BUTTER-SAUTÉED MUSHROOM AND ONION BURGERS MADE FROM FRESH GROUND BEEF CHUCK. OR WHISKEY BACON AND EGG CHEESEBURGERS—ALSO KNOWN AS HANGOVER BURGERS. CALL IT WHAT YOU WANT, IT'S ALL GOOD EATING AT THE PIT.

MUSHROOM & ONION HAMBURGERS

INGREDIENTS

- 1 lb roast ground beef chuck
- ¼ small to medium onion, chopped
- ¼ cup mushrooms, sliced
- SPG seasoning
- 1 tbsp butter
- 2 slices bread

PITMASTER TIP

If you do not want to grind your own meat, have the butcher or meat counter at your store grind it for you.

Sick of those plain old grilled hamburgers? Try this butter-sautéed mushroom and onion burger made from fresh ground beef chuck. It's easy to do!

METHOD

1 Grind the chuck roast, if you're doing it yourself.

2 Form the ground chuck into a 1 lb patty—you want to make the patty firm and tight so it will not fall apart on the grill.

3 Season the patty with SPG, to taste.

4 Set up your grill for indirect heat (hot coals on one side of the grill and no coals on the other side)—you're looking for medium hot coals.

5 Place skillet over the coals and add a dab of butter.

6 Add the onions and mushrooms to the skillet to sauté them, then cover grill with the lid.

7 After the onions and mushrooms begin to brown—it just takes a few minutes—move the skillet to the side of the grill with no coals (indirect heat).

8 Place the ground chuck patty on the grill directly over the hot coals to sear the burger, then re-cover the grill with its lid. The burger needs about 2 minutes each side.

9 After the burger is seared, move it to the side of the grill with no coals to finish cooking.

10 Cook the burger to the doneness that you prefer.

11 Place the burger on one of the slices of bread and top with the mushrooms, onions, and butter from the skillet.

12 Top with the second slice of bread. Divide in half to share.

13 Serve and enjoy!

I've got my Barbecue shoes on!

HELL BURGER BACON CHEESEBURGER

INGREDIENTS

- 4 lb ground beef chuck, 80/20 (meat/fat)
- SPG seasoning, to taste
- 4 jalapeños, sliced
- 1 onion, sliced and grilled
- pepper relish, favorite brand or homemade
- hot sauce, to taste
- cayenne pepper, to taste
- ½ lb thick cut bacon, cooked
- 1½ cups mozzarella, shredded
- 1½ cup cheddar, shredded
- hamburger buns
- favorite condiments

The hotter she is the better...check out this hamburger recipe from hell to serve up hot off your grill. She's hot—just the way we like her!

METHOD

1 Bring grill temperature up to 375°F, with coals offset for indirect cooking.

2 Make 3 x 1⅓ lb burger patties.

3 Season both sides with SPG.

4 Sear burgers on both sides directly over hot coals.

5 Move burgers opposite hot coals to finish cooking. Cook to desired doneness.

6 Pile high with jalapeños, grilled onions, pepper relish, bacon, cayenne pepper, hot sauce, mozzarella, and cheddar cheese (to personal taste).

7 Cover the grill and allow the cheese to melt.

8 Remove burgers from the grill and place on the buns.

9 Top with any other favorite condiments.

10 Serve with smoked beans, coleslaw, potato salad, and a cold beverage.

11 Sit back, relax, and enjoy!

SCAN & WATCH

So hot she'll blow your mind!

SCAN & WATCH

DOUBLE CHEESE BACON-BANG BURGERS

INGREDIENTS

- 1 lb ground beef chuck
- cheddar cheese
- bacon, grilled
- SPG seasoning
- sweet onions, grilled
- mushrooms, grilled
- 2 burger buns

PITMASTER PRIVILEGE

You can use whatever toppings you like on these burgers.

Loaded with beef, bacon, cheese, mushrooms, and sweet onions, you'll need a flip-top head to get this in but that's half the fun. Go ahead and treat yourself.

METHOD

1 Mix SPG or your favorite seasoning into the chuck burger meat, then form into 4 patties.

2 Put 2 patties into a plastic bag, and then double-bag it.

3 Using a meat mallet, bang the burger meat until very flat and approximate size of a very large dinner plate. Repeat with the other two burger patties.

4 Divide the flattened chuck in half, and form again into two patties. Repeat for remaining chuck meat so you have four pounded chuck patties.

5 Bring grill temperature to 325°F.

6 Place the burgers on the grill over hot coals, cook for a few minutes, then flip the burgers.

7 After flipping the burgers, pile cheddar cheese on top and leave to cook for a few more minutes.

8 Once cooked, stack two of the patties on a burger bun, layering the bacon, onions, and mushrooms in between the patties and on top.

9 Sit back and enjoy!

BACON CHEESEBURGER DELUXE

INGREDIENTS

- 4 lb ground beef chuck, 80/20 (meat/fat)
- SPG seasoning, to taste
- 1 lb shredded cheese, divided in half
- 3 cans tomato paste (or a homemade sauce)

SUGGESTED TOPPINGS

- 1 lb bacon, thick sliced
- 8 oz pepperoni
- 2–3 links (12 oz) sausage, removed from natural casings and sliced
- 1–2 oz olives, sliced
- 4–6 mushrooms, sliced
- 1 red bell pepper, sliced
- 1 white onion, thick sliced
- 2 garlic cloves, minced
- 4 jalapeños, divided—2 sliced, 2 finely diced
- 1–2 sprigs parsley, chopped
- 8 hamburger buns
- pickles, onion, tomato to garnish

PITMASTER PRIVILEGE

You can use any toppings you like, whatever you have in the refrigerator. Use your imagination!

Made with 80/20 ground beef and served on a crispy bun, this burger will leave you craving for more. Savor the irresistible flavors of juicy meat and crispy bacon, topped with melted cheese, lettuce, and tomato. Welcome to burger paradise!

METHOD

1 Bring grill temperature up to 275°F, with coals offset for indirect cooking.

2 Combine SPG with ground chuck in a 2" deep grill-safe pan. Mix well together, then flatten out over the entire pan.

3 Spread the tomato paste or sauce evenly all over the meat and sprinkle half of the shredded cheese over the meat.

4 Layer the toppings (as suggested here or whatever you prefer) evenly all over the meat base.

5 Place the pan opposite hot coals for indirect cooking and cover the grill. Cook for 45 minutes, then remove excess grease from pan using a turkey baster. You may have to do this more than once depending on your meat.

6 Rotate the pan for even cooking. Cover and cook another 45 minutes.

7 Meanwhile, combine the garlic and jalapeños. Set aside.

8 When finished cooking, carefully slice the loaf into 8 pieces while still on the grill.

9 Top each piece with additional shredded cheese, then add the jalapeño and garlic mixture on top.

10 Cover and cook until the cheese has melted, 10 minutes.

11 Remove the burgers from the pan and place on hamburger buns. Top with onion, pickles, tomatoes, or any other favorites.

12 Serve with smoked beans, coleslaw, or potato salad.

13 Sit back, relax, and enjoy!

Welcome to burger paradise!

BEER CAN BACON BURGER

INGREDIENTS

- 4–5 lb ground beef chuck, 80/20 (meat/fat), kept cold
- 2 lb bacon, pork belly, regular cut
- 1 can beer, unopened
- 10 buns

FOR THE STUFFING/TOPPING

- cheese (your favorite will do), chunked/shredded
- mushrooms, chopped
- onions, grilled and chopped
- red/green bell peppers, chopped
- tomato, chopped
- bacon, chopped
- roast beef, chopped
- beef hash
- canned chili
- BBQ sauce
- hot sauce

Stuff 'em with what you like! Don't let us tell you how good these burgers are, find out why over 7 million people enjoyed this video, now unofficially referred to as America's greatest burger.

METHOD

1 Bring grill temperature up to 300°F with coals offset for indirect cooking.

2 Sauté mushrooms, onions, and peppers.

3 Grill the chopped tomato, bacon, roast beef, beef hash, and canned chili (or other favorite toppings) until they are hot.

4 Make hamburger balls, 8 to 12 oz each. Make sure the meat is cold.

5 Press beer can deep into center of each meatball, forming a pocket around the can.

6 Wrap bacon around each ball of ground chuck. Each one should take two pieces of bacon.

7 Using a dish towel, carefully remove beer can from meatball.

8 Continue until all meatballs have been formed.

9 Choose some stuffing/toppings and place them inside the meatball pockets, followed by 2–3 cheese chunks or a layer of shredded cheese.

10 Add a few dashes of hot sauce or BBQ sauce.

11 Place bacon burgers opposite hot coals for indirect cooking. Put lid on the grill and cook for one hour. You may need to turn and rotate after 30 minutes.

12 When cooked to your liking, remove from the grill.

13 Place the burgers on the buns and top with your favorite condiments.

14 Serve with fries, chips, coleslaw, potato salad, or grilled vegetables.

15 Sit back, relax, and enjoy!

BBQ PIT BOYS

...And—Through the Miracle of Time...

STEAK 'N' BACON CHEESEBURGER

INGREDIENTS

- **2 lb ground beef chuck**
- **SPG seasoning (or some salt and pepper)**
- **1 boneless rib eye roast**
- **4–8 bacon slices, smoked**
- **4 cheese slices**
- **1 onion, thinly sliced**
- **4 burger buns**
- **your favorite burger condiments**

Kick up that ordinary burger you've been making with this easy to do steak burger. It's real good eating at the Pit with these few simple steps by the BBQ Pit Boys.

METHOD

1 Press the ground beef out flat on a board, to about half an inch thickness. Sprinkle the seasoning on the ground beef, lift one side of the beef to fold in on itself, then combine well.

2 Form four large, half-inch-deep patties and place them on the grill with indirect heat. Cook until the meat reaches a minimum temperature of 160°F, flipping once.

3 Thinly slice the boneless rib eye roast steaks and season only one side of each steak.

4 When the burgers are almost done, place the steaks directly over very hot coals for a fast cook. You only need to cook one side of the steak face down over the coals; just flip it once to remove any moisture that formed on top, and resist the temptation to sear this side or it will be overcooked.

5 Place the cheese on the beef burgers, then place the steak on the cheese, topping off with the bacon. Finally, add the sliced onion and your favorite condiments, then top it off with the burger bun lid. To share, slice in half.

6 Serve and enjoy!

BACON VEGGIE BURGERS

INGREDIENTS

- 3½ lb ground beef chuck, 80/20 (meat/fat)
- 1½ lb ground pork or sausage meat
- 1 lb bacon slices
- 1 red pepper, cleaned and chopped
- 1 onion, chopped/sliced
- 5–10 pimento stuffed olives, chopped
- jalapeño peppers—pickled or fresh, sliced
- 1 can mushroom pieces
- 3–4 oz salami slices
- 1 lb mozzarella cheese, shredded
- salt, to taste
- 1 tbsp black pepper, to taste
- lettuce
- 1 tomato, sliced
- 12 burger buns
- your favorite burger condiments
- wax paper

Momma always said, "eat your vegetables," so we do with this grilled bacon-wrapped veggie burger, BBQ Pit Boys style. If you like veggies, check out this recipe.

METHOD

1 Bring grill temperature up to 300°F, with coals on one side for indirect cooking.

2 Place bacon in half pound slabs on the grill opposite hot coals for indirect cooking. Cover and cook 10–15 minutes.

3 Flip the bacon, cover and cook for another 10 minutes until half cooked, then remove from the grill. With the lid on, raise the grill temperature to 350°F–400°F.

4 Combine ground chuck and pork (or sausage meat) in a bowl, season with salt and pepper, to taste. Mix well.

5 On the wax paper, form 2–2½ lb of meat mixture into a 7" x 12" rectangle, a half inch thick, then scatter the vegetables, salami, and mozzarella over the meat base.

6 Lift one edge of the wax paper to raise the meat, carefully rolling the meat into a log.

7 Cut the log into 7 rounds. Wrap a slice of the half cooked bacon around each veggie patty, and place the burgers opposite the hot coals to cook for 8–10 minutes with the grill covered.

8 Remove the lid to flip the burgers and place any leftover bacon directly over the hot coals to finish cooking. Re-cover the grill and cook for another 5–10 minutes, then move away from the coals for indirect cooking.

9 After 5–10 minutes, check the internal temperature of the burgers; they will be done once they reach 160°F.

10 Add cheese to each veggie patty, cover grill and allow to melt for 3–5 minutes, then remove from grill and top with a slice of bacon and more veggies.

11 Serve with your favorite condiments and sides, sit back, relax, and enjoy!

What good is a veggie burger without another layer of bacon?...

SCAN & WATCH

Oh me, oh my!

WHISKEY BACON & EGG CHEESEBURGERS

INGREDIENTS

FOR THE PATTY

- ¾ lb ground beef chuck (as needed)
- SPG seasoning (or salt and pepper), to taste
- 2 bacon slices, smoked
- shredded cheese, to taste

FOR THE GRAVY

- 2 tbsp butter
- 3 garlic cloves, minced
- ¼ cup minced onion
- seasoning blend, to taste
- 2 oz whiskey (2–4 shots if desired)
- 4 cups beef broth
- 2 tbsp flour, dissolved in a little cold water

FOR SERVING

- 2 bread slices, toasted
- 2 fried eggs

Some call this the hangover burger. Call it what you want but it's still good eating at the Pit.

METHOD

1 Roll meat into 3 equal sized burger patties and season with SPG or salt and pepper.

2 Cook burgers over direct heat until partially cooked, then move off the coals to continue cooking indirectly.

3 Place a pan on the grill and crumble a burger into it. Add the butter, garlic, and onion and cook for a few minutes. Add seasoning and stir well.

4 Add whiskey and beef broth. Boil for 15–20 minutes.

5 Gradually stir some water into the flour and stir to a paste. Pour the mixture into the gravy, stirring well. Cook until the gravy is thickened.

6 Top the remaining two patties with smoked bacon slices and cheese. Cover and cook until the cheese melts.

7 Fry two eggs as you like 'em.

8 Top a slice of bread with a cheeseburger, followed by a fried egg, and then pour gravy over the top.

9 Top with a second slice of bread, serve and enjoy!

POTATO CHIP BACON BURGERS

INGREDIENTS

- 5–6 lb ground beef chuck 80/20 (meat/fat)
- 1 lb bacon, thick sliced, pork belly style
- 1–2 tbsp brown sugar
- SPG seasoning, to taste
- 1 large bag potato chips, your favorite flavor
- 12–15 hamburger buns
- pickles, sliced
- onions, sliced
- tomato, sliced
- cheese slices
- your favorite condiments

PITMASTER PRIVILEGE

Here at the Pit we like to add some whole potato chips on top of the garnishes in our burgers—for that extra crunch! Ooooh yeah!

Potato chips and hamburgers are the perfect combo for any picnic or food feast, and now we know why. Check out how the BBQ Pit Boys make 'em.

METHOD

1 Bring grill temperature up to 250°F–300°F, with coals offset for indirect cooking.

2 Divide the bacon into ¼ lb slabs and put them on the grill opposite the coals for indirect cooking. Sprinkle with brown sugar and add some wood to the charcoal for smoking. Cover grill. After 45 minutes, add some more wood.

3 After an hour, turn the bacon for even cooking. Cover grill and smoke for another hour. Remove bacon and set aside.

4 Separate ground chuck into ⅓ lb burgers.

5 Take favorite potato chips and crush ½ oz for each burger.

6 Squash the chips into the meat until well combined.

7 Flatten the balls of meat into half-inch deep patties using a burger press. Season each patty with SPG seasoning.

8 Increase grill's temperature to 325°F–350°F.

9 Place burgers directly over hot coals and cover the grill. Cook for 3–4 minutes, then uncover the grill and flip the burgers. Cover again and cook for another 3–4 minutes. Be sure the chips don't burn.

10 Remove the burgers from the grill once they reach desired doneness and place on buns.

11 Top with some smoked bacon, cheese, onions, pickles, tomatoes, or any of your favorite toppings and condiments.

12 Serve with pit beans, coleslaw, or any of the sides recipes (see pages 214–223) and your favorite potato chips, of course.

13 Sit back, relax, and enjoy!

Oh LORD have mercy!

REAPER GHOST CHEESEBURGER

INGREDIENTS

- 4 fresh ghost peppers
- 2 fresh Carolina reapers
- 8 stalks of green onion
- 3 cloves garlic
- 1 lb partially cooked bacon
- 2 lb ground sirloin steak
- 1 tbsp of SPG seasoning
- 4 tsp of brown sugar

FOR THE CHEESE SAUCE

- 1 cup milk
- 4 tbsp flour
- 2 cups pepper jack cheese

Don't fear the reaper. Light it up with this classic hot chili pepper cheeseburger by the BBQ Pit Boys. It comes with the South Carolina reaper, known as the hottest pepper on the planet, and the ghost pepper. These burgers are packed with flavor and topped with a jack cheese sauce. Your family and friends will luv 'em.

METHOD

1 Remove the seeds from the chilies.

2 Finely chop the peppers, green onions, and garlic.

3 Finely chop the bacon. The fat from the bacon will go well with the lean ground sirloin, which has a 90/10 fat ratio.

4 Combine the meat, vegetables, brown sugar, and the SPG seasoning and mix well.

5 Place the mix into the fridge for about an hour.

6 To make the cheese sauce, combine ingredients in a pot over medium heat and stir continuously until smooth.

7 Form the burger patties.

8 Place the burgers on the grill over direct heat to sear, then move them to indirect heat and cover. Cook to an internal temperature of 160°F.

9 Serve on a toasted burger bun topped with the cheese sauce and your favorite toppings.

BEEF BACON LIVER BURGERS

INGREDIENTS

- 2 lb ground beef chuck
- 1 lb liver
- 2 cups whole milk
- olive oil
- 1 tbsp SPG seasoning
- ½ cup jalapeños
- 1 tsp of smoked paprika
- ½ cup brown sugar
- 1 tbsp garlic powder
- 1 tbsp marjoram
- 8 slices thick-sliced bacon
- 8 slices of pepper jack cheese
- 1 extra large onion
- 1 tbsp butter
- 6 ciabatta bread rolls
- mayonnaise
- olive oil
- your favorite toppings

If you like liver then you have to check this recipe out. The BBQ Pit Boys tenderize the beef liver in milk, grind it, and add in some chuck ground beef, bacon and onions...and it's real easy to do.

METHOD

1 Cut the liver into ½ inch slices.

2 Place the liver in a ziplock bag or a bowl, cover with milk and let it soak overnight in the fridge for at least 8 hours. Once the soak has finished, rinse off and pat dry with a paper towel.

3 Grind down or finely chop the liver, add it to the 2 lb of ground chuck, and place the mix into the refrigerator. Chop up the bacon into 1 inch pieces and fry them in a pan; take the bacon out before it's crispy.

4 Dice up the onion and place a tablespoon or so of butter and a splash of olive oil into the bacon drippings. Fry them until caramelized/browned.

5 Add the SPG seasoning, marjoram, bacon, fried onions, brown sugar, jalapeños, smoked paprika, and garlic powder to the beef and liver and mix well by hand. Form the mix into 1 lb patties, more or less—you can choose how big to make them.

6 Fire up a bed of coals until good and hot and place the formed burgers over direct heat to sear.

7 Once seared on both sides, move them to indirect heat. Once they reach an internal temp of at least 155°F, add the sliced pepper jack cheese and continue the cook until the cheese has melted.

8 Toast the ciabatta rolls, spread on some mayonnaise, and serve the burgers with your favorite toppings.

SCAN & WATCH

BBQ PIT BOYS

It's about time to eat!

38

JALAPEÑO BACON CHUCK BURGERS

INGREDIENTS

- 5 lb beef chuck roast, coarse ground, or fresh coarse ground chuck from your local butcher
- 1 lb bacon, smoked
- 8 oz jalapeño peppers, seeded and diced (about 4–5 peppers)
- ¾ cup onion, chopped
- 1 tbsp SPG seasoning
- 2 tbsp Worcestershire sauce
- 1 tsp cayenne pepper
- ¼ cup pepper jack or chipotle cheese, diced small
- hamburger buns
- your favorite condiments

TO SMOKE THE BACON

Place the bacon on the grill over low indirect heat, cover, and cook for about 40 minutes, flipping halfway through.

Fresh ground beef chuck burgers cooked up on the grill is about as good as good eatin' gets.

METHOD

1 Put your chuck roast in the freezer to firm up so that it will be easier to grind.

2 Cut the roast into 1 inch cubes and grind it to a coarse grind.

3 Set up your grill for indirect heat (hot coals on one side of the grill and no coals on the other side of the grill).

4 In a bowl mix the ground chuck roast, jalapeño peppers, onion, SPG seasoning, the Worcestershire sauce, cayenne pepper, and the pepper jack or chipotle cheese.

5 Form the mixture into ½ lb patties about ¾ inch thick.

6 Place the burgers directly over the hot coals and sear each side of the burger for 2 minutes.

7 Then move the burgers to the side of the grill with no coals and cover grill with the lid. Cook burgers to your desired doneness.

8 Add pepper jack cheese to the top of the burgers and let melt.

9 Place each burger on a bun and top with smoked bacon.

10 Add your favorite condiments.

11 Serve and enjoy!

SCAN & WATCH

"Going down to the house of sausage."

BACON PIG DOGS IN A BLANKET

INGREDIENTS

- 1 lb smoked thick sliced bacon
- 2 lb ground pork
- 6 hot dogs or smoked frankfurters
- 6 sheets flaky pastry
- 1 cup breadcrumbs
- ½ cup fine grated carrot
- 1 cup grated sharp cheese
- ¾ cup of grated onion, patted dry to remove moisture
- 1 tbsp fresh ground black pepper
- 1 tbsp salt
- English mustard
- ketchup
- sesame seeds
- SPG seasoning, or your favorite seasoning
- 1 egg
- 1 tbsp water

Pigs in a blanket with a much improved BBQ Pit Boys twist. Wrapped in ground pork and packed with tasty cheese and diced smoked bacon then wrapped in flaky pastry, these bacon pig dogs in a blanket will have them coming back for more, so you better make a bunch.

Pigs in a blanket gone wild, get this pork on ya fork ASAP, these bacon pig dogs in a blanket are a game changer.

METHOD

1 Smoke the bacon over indirect heat to your preferred level of doneness and dice.

2 Combine the ground pork, breadcrumbs, ½ cup of grated sharp cheese, SPG seasoning, grated onion, fresh ground black pepper, and salt.

3 Spread about a tablespoon of ketchup across the middle of a sheet of flaky pastry.

4 Place a layer of the ground pork mixture onto the ketchup strip on the pastry.

5 Place a layer of diced smoked bacon onto the ground pork mix.

6 Place a hot dog/frankfurter onto the bacon and add some mustard.

7 Top with more of the ground pork mix.

8 Roll the pastry around the pork mix, brushing the inside of one end of the pastry with the egg wash (1 egg, 1 tbsp water), and seal the roll with light pressure and more egg wash. Repeat until all 6 pigs in blankets are prepared.

9 Sprinkle with sesame seeds, and they're ready for the grill.

10 Place onto a sheet of parchment paper on an oven tray and place on a preheated grill over indirect heat at 350°F.

11 Cook until the rolls reach an internal temperature of 165°F. Rotate for even cooking about halfway through.

12 Add the remaining grated cheese and diced smoked bacon topping just before the rolls are finished cooking.

13 Serve hot, with ketchup.

SCAN & WATCH

Are you kidding me?!

GRILLED SAUSAGE 'N' PEPPERS SUB

INGREDIENTS

- 10 fresh sausages in natural casing
- 9–10 bell peppers, mixed colors
- 2 loaves French bread
- fresh basil (optional)
- 2 medium onions, chopped large
- 4–6 garlic cloves, crushed
- olive oil
- SPG seasoning (or your favorite seasoning)

Need a good last minute recipe? Grilled sausage, peppers, and onions on a fresh bread roll is hard to beat, whether at your pit, the carnival, or the tailgate party. Make a few up using the simple tips and tricks below.

METHOD

1 Preheat the grill to about 350°F, set up for indirect cooking—with coals on one side only.

2 Place the sausages on the grill away from the coals, over indirect heat.

3 While the sausages cook, cut the onion into large pieces, cut the peppers in half, and remove the seeds.

4 Place the green peppers over direct heat to char the skins. Don't be afraid to get a good char, you want this flavor profile.

5 Put a pan on the grill to heat up, add the olive oil, then add the onions and garlic. Fry them just a little; they still need some crunch. Add some SPG seasoning toward the end.

6 Add the remaining bell peppers to the grill to char the outsides. When ready, flip them over to roast them—this side won't char because of the shape of the peppers.

7 When ready, take the roasted peppers off the grill, chop them roughly, and add to the pan with the onion and garlic.

8 Slice the sausages lengthwise and add to the pan. Meanwhile, warm two loaves of French bread on the grill.

9 If desired, add fresh basil to the pan to heat through and impart its flavor into the mix.

10 Serve on a good crusty baguette. You may want to butter the bread first, but that's optional.

BBQ SAUSAGE SANDWICH

INGREDIENTS

- 2 lb (3 feet) natural casing sausage
- 4 tbsp rub (as needed)
- 1 lb bacon slices
- 1 onion, sliced, rings separated
- 4 green bell peppers, sliced
- 2 tbsp cooking oil
- 1 cup shredded mozzarella
- 2 large buns or small round loaves
- skewers

Check out this easy to do, slow-cooked pork sausage, bacon, pepper, onion, and cheese sandwich.

METHOD

1 Preheat grill to 250°F–275°F.

2 Make a swirl of the sausage and insert a couple of skewers to hold the shape.

3 Season both sides of the sausage and bacon with the rub. Place the sausage and bacon at a point of indirect heat on the grill.

4 Cover and allow to bake for 2 to 2½ hours, flipping when required. Once cooked, lay the bacon slices on top of the sausage swirl.

5 Place a pan on the grill over the hot coals, add oil, onion, and bell peppers, sauté for few minutes until softened, and place on top of the bacon.

6 Top with the mozzarella, cover the grill, and cook until the cheese has melted.

7 Divide the bun horizontally in half and lightly core out.

8 Place the sausage on the bun, remove the skewer, and place the bun back on the grill. Cook until toasted.

9 Cut the bun in half and serve with your choice of beverage.

This here is what we call—Pitmaster's Privilege!

BBQ PIT BOYS

SCAN & WATCH

Man it smells. GUUUD already!

GRILLED KIELBASA SAUSAGE

INGREDIENTS

FOR THE SANDWICH

- 1 large fresh kielbasa sausage (approx. 1½ lb)
- 12 cups fresh packaged sauerkraut
- 2 tbsp whole black peppercorns
- 1 small sweet onion, chopped
- hot dog buns
- your favorite condiments

TO SERVE

- boiled white potatoes
- butter
- fresh apple sauce
- pickled cabbage

PITMASTER PRIVILEGE

This sausage could be beef sausage, lamb sausage, or veal sausage—depends where on this planet you're from.

Kielbasa Polish sausage, with slow grilled peppercorn sauerkraut piled high on a sandwich, or simply served alongside buttered boiled potatoes!

METHOD

1 Preheat the grill to about 300°F–325°F .

2 Add peppercorns and the chopped onion to the sauerkraut.

3 Sear the kielbasa sausage on the grill—about 2 minutes each side. Then cut it up into about 4–5 inch lengths.

4 Add the sausage lengths to the pan and bury them in the sauerkraut. Cover and cook for an hour.

5 Turn the pan around on the grill to ensure even cooking.

6 After another half an hour or so, this is DONE!

7 Serve with sides of boiled potatoes with butter, apple sauce, and pickled cabbage.

SCAN &
WATCH

It's HOT
in the kitchen!

BISON SAUSAGE & KRAUT SANDWICH

INGREDIENTS

- 3 lb bison sausages
- 6 oz beer
- 2 lb fresh sauerkraut
- 1–2 tbsp fresh ground black pepper
- 4 large hot dog buns
- mustard for serving

Grilled bison sausage slow simmered in beer and sauerkraut and then served on a bun is good eating at its best here at the Pit.

METHOD

1 Sear the bison sausages—a couple of minutes on each side over the coals of a medium-hot grill.

2 Move the sausages to a deep cast-iron pan on the other side of the grill.

3 Pour the beer into the pan, put the pan on the grill over the coals, then pile the sauerkraut on top of the sausages. Sprinkle the ground black pepper over the sauerkraut and stir to combine.

4 Cover the grill and leave to steam over indirect heat for half an hour.

5 After 15 minutes, stir everything together until thoroughly combined, re-cover the grill, and cook for 15 more minutes.

6 When ready, split the buns and fill with the sausage and sauerkraut mixture.

7 Serve with mustard. Sit back and enjoy!

PEPPERED PORK BACON BUTTER BURGER

INGREDIENTS

- 1 lb pork belly bacon rashers
- 1 lb ground pork
- ½ stick butter
- your favorite sauce
- burger buns
- cheese slices
- onions, finely shredded
- smoked paprika
- sea salt
- coarse black pepper, to taste
- tomatoes, sliced
- mayonnaise

PITMASTER PRIVILEGE

Enjoy your tasty peppered pork bacon butter burger dressed up with soft sautéed onions, sliced tomatoes, and any other of your favorite condiments.

This peppered pork bacon butter burger is packing a ton of flavor and won't let you down like those fast food burgers always do, so be sure to make a bunch of these.

METHOD

1 Heat some oil in a pan over the hot coals of the grill. Add the shredded onions and some salt and fry until the onions are soft. Set aside.

2 Chop the pork belly bacon finely. Add some smoked paprika, some sauce, the butter, and the ground pork. Mix everything together well.

3 Form the mixed meat into burger patties. Flatten each burger a little and sprinkle a large amount of coarse black pepper all over one side. Make a small dip in the center of each burger.

4 Start the burgers on indirect heat for a few minutes, then move them above the coals. Cook the underneath of the burger the way you want it before you flip it; you want to preserve as much of the black pepper as possible.

5 In the meantime, toast some burger buns on the grill away from the coals.

6 Flip the burgers to briefly sear the underside, then turn them right side up, add a slice of cheese, cover the grill, and let the cheese melt a little.

7 Take the toasted buns off the grill and spread mayonnaise (or whatever condiments you like) over the bottom bun.

8 Place the burger with cheese on the buns, dressing them up with the fried onions, tomato, or anything else you like.

9 Sit back and enjoy!

SCAN &
WATCH

BBQ PIT BOYS
It don't get any better than this!

MEATLOAF, MEATBALLS & PIES

AND THROUGH THE MIRACLE OF TIME, WE HAVE EVOLVED FROM THE CLASSICS—BARBECUE BURGERS AND STEAKS—TO BBQ PIES! WHO WOULD HAVE THOUGHT OF THAT? THE PIT BOYS, THAT'S WHO. THERE'S NOTHING WE WON'T TRY, AS YOU'LL SEE THROUGHOUT THIS BOOK. DOWN AT THE PIT, GOOD EATING IS OUR RELIGION.

MEATLOAF HAMBURGER SUPREME

INGREDIENTS

- 3–4 lb beef, ground chuck (or 80% beef)
- 3–5 slices bacon
- 1 lb pork sausage, casing removed, sausage pieces
- 2 large bell peppers
- 1 large onion, sliced
- pepperoni
- sliced mushrooms
- sliced pineapple
- shredded cheese
- your favorite beef spices
- BBQ sauce or tomato sauce

Now here's a real easy-to-do recipe for beef meatloaf with "the works": all cooked on the backyard grill!

METHOD

1 Form and flatten the beef ground chuck on a baking pan about 1–2 inches thick. Add your favorite spices.

2 Sauté sausage and bacon, then add sliced vegetables, cooking only slightly so that they remain firm.

3 Spread the sauce on the meatloaf, then cover with your favorite shredded cheese.

4 Cover the meatloaf with all the prepared sausage, bacon, and veggies. Add pepperoni and pineapple slices.

5 Place the loaf opposite the hot coals in a grill set up for indirect heat.

6 Add some hickory wood, apple wood, or mesquite to produce a light smoke (optional).

7 Maintain temperature of the covered grill at around 250°F–275°F for up to about 1hour, or until the internal temperature of the meatloaf reaches about 165°F.

8 Remove, slice into burger patties, serve, and enjoy.

SCAN & WATCH

Life is GUUUD
at the Pit!

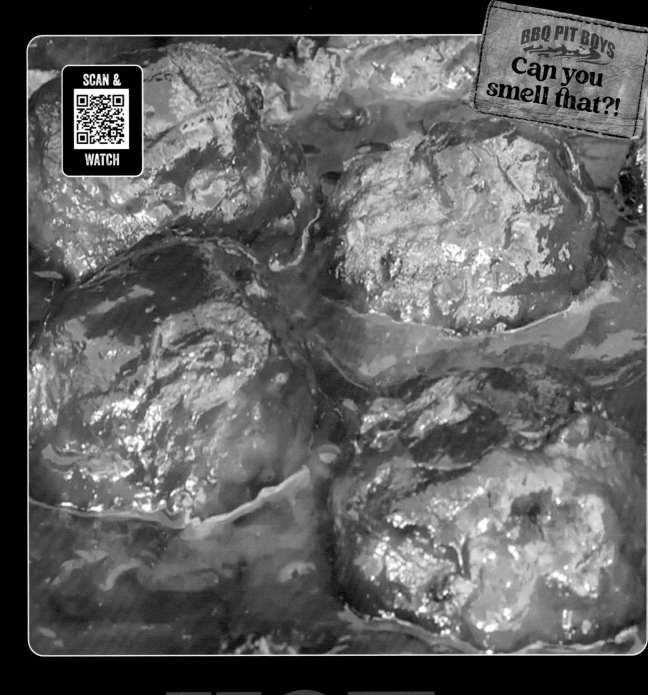

SCAN &
WATCH

BBQ PIT BOYS
Can you smell that?!

It's HOT
in the kitchen!

SERVES: 8 | PREP TIME: 20 MINUTES | COOK TIME: 1 HOUR

BBQ MEATBALLS

INGREDIENTS

- **4 lb ground chuck**
- **1 small onion, diced**
- **1 egg**
- **2 garlic cloves, minced**
- **½ tsp garlic powder**
- **1 tsp fresh ground black pepper**
- **½ tsp salt**
- **½ cup grated parmesan cheese**
- **¼ cup breadcrumbs**
- **¼ cup milk**
- **2 cups BBQ sauce**

FOR SERVING

- **8 sandwich rolls**

These easy-to-make beef meatballs are slowly simmered in BBQ sauce for some real guuud eatin'.

METHOD

1 Preheat grill.

2 In a dish, mix together ground chuck, onion, egg, garlic, garlic powder, pepper, salt, half the parmesan, and breadcrumbs.

3 Add milk and mix again, then form the mix into meatballs.

4 Place the meatballs on the grill over direct heat and sear from both sides.

5 Once seared, transfer to a pan placed over indirect heat, cover with sauce, cover, and cook at 300°F for about an hour.

6 Place 3 meatballs in a sandwich roll, pour in some sauce, and sprinkle with the remaining cheese.

7 Place the sandwich on the grill at indirect heat and toast until the cheese is melted. Drizzle with some more sauce.

8 Serve with beer or your choice of beverage.

BBQ PIT BOYS
GUUUD eating
at the Pit!!

PEPPERONI PIZZA PIE

INGREDIENTS

FOR THE PIZZA BASE

- pizza dough
- olive oil
- 1 cup cornmeal
- 1 jar of tomato sauce
- SPG seasoning (or salt and pepper), to taste

FOR THE TOPPING

- good quality pepperoni
- 8 oz mozzarella cheese
- 8 oz cheddar cheese
- 1 tbsp garlic powder
- 1 tbsp red pepper flakes (or more if you like)
- whole leaf basil (optional)
- whole leaf oregano
- parmesan cheese, grated

Your great grandma's old school pizza pie, the way it should still be done. Check out how easy it is to make your own, and not have to settle for the chain delivered bread with pepperoni, cheese, and sauce.

METHOD

1 Sprinkle and rub flour over your work area and turn out the pizza dough on to the floured surface.

2 Stretch the pizza dough ball in all directions, lifting it and turning it in the air so it becomes more of a sheet of dough rather than a ball.

3 On the floured surface roll the sheet of dough length and width-wise into a rectangle or circle (depending on the shape of pizza tray you're using) with a rolling pin.

4 Lightly oil the pizza tray and sprinkle cornmeal over the oil.

5 Press and stretch the dough up to the edges of the pizza tray, and slightly up the sides for a raised edge to the crust. Season the base with SPG or salt and pepper.

6 Spoon on and smear tomato sauce all over the pizza base.

7 Sprinkle the cheeses evenly all over the tomato base, followed by the garlic powder and pepper flakes.

8 Thinly slice the pepperoni sausage and place on the top of the pizza. Use as much or as little as you like.

9 Lay some basil and oregano leaves amongst the pepperoni, if using.

10 Rub some olive oil all along the raised edge of the crust to ensure a good crunchy crust. Sprinkle on more parmesan.

11 Cook in a wood fired oven at 600°F–650°F. Or using a kettle oven, indirect, opposite the coals.

12 After 10–15 minutes rotate the pizza if necessary.

13 When it's ready, remove from the pizza tray, cut into pieces and share with friends. Enjoy!

SCAN &
WATCH

Man!
that tastes
GUUUD...

GRILLED BEEF POT PIE

INGREDIENTS

FOR GRAVY

- 2–5 slices bacon
- 2 tbsp onion, chopped
- 2 tbsp sweet butter
- 3 tbsp flour
- ¼ cup wine or beer
- roast beef drippings (optional) or use extra beef broth
- 1½ cups beef broth
- 1 tsp SPG seasoning
- cast iron pot

FOR PIE

- 1½–2 lb tender cooked roast beef or steak
- ¼ cup celery, diced
- 3 tbsp onion, chopped
- 6 potatoes, cooked and cut into bite-sized pieces
- 2 carrots, sliced and cooked
- 2 prepared pie dough crusts
- butter

PITMASTER PRIVILEGE

You can also use meatballs as the meat filling for this pie. They work great!

On a cold winter's night no food warms the soul better than a big serving of Beef Pot Pie.

METHOD: GRAVY

1 Set up your grill for indirect heat (hot coals on one side of the grill only). You're looking for a grill temperature of 425°F.

2 Place your cast-iron pan over the coals for direct grilling.

3 Cut up 2 slices of bacon and put into the pan—the rendered bacon fat will start as the base of your gravy.

4 Add chopped onion into the pan to sauté in the fat.

5 Add sweet butter—you are starting to make a roux to help thicken up the gravy.

6 Dust flour into the pan, stirring constantly until fully incorporated.

7 Add wine or beer to the pan, followed by roast beef drippings, beef broth, and SPG seasoning. If roast drippings are not available, add extra beef broth.

8 Move the pan over indirect heat, stir the gravy to mix, and let simmer to thicken for a few minutes.

9 After gravy thickens, add celery.

10 Cut tender cooked roast beef into bite-sized pieces and add to the pan.

11 Put chopped onion into the pot, along with the precooked potatoes and carrots.

12 Stir and let simmer.

METHOD: THE PIE

13 Roll out 1 of the prepared pie doughs and place into an oven-safe pie plate. Scoop the gravy evenly into the pie crust.

14 Roll out the second prepared pie dough and place on top of the filling. Seal the edges, then cut slits into the top pie crust to release steam.

15 Place the pie plate over indirect heat, cover the grill, and cook for 15 minutes. Rotate the pie 180°, rub the top crust with butter (to brown). Re-cover and cook for another 15 minutes, then remove.

16 Let the pie rest for 30 minutes to let the crust firm up, then serve and enjoy!

CHEESE & BACON MEATBALL SUB

INGREDIENTS

- 2 lb ground beef
- 2 lb ground pork
- 1 tbsp SPG
- 1 onion, diced
- ½ lb bacon
- ½ cup BBQ sauce
- 2 cups diced tomatoes
- 2 cups tomato sauce
- 2 cups tomato puree
- 2 tbsp ketchup
- 1 cup meat sauce (we used a mix of smoked turkey and chicken whipped up in a blender)
- 1 tbsp onion powder
- 2 tbsp onion flakes
- 2 tbsp Italian seasoning
- 1 tbsp garlic powder
- salt and pepper, to taste
- 1 egg
- cheddar cheese
- 8 bread rolls

It's super-easy to make these cheese and bacon meatball subs. Your family and friends will love them, so be sure to make a bunch, and don't skimp on the cheese!

METHOD

1 Combine all tomato ingredients, BBQ sauce, ketchup, meat sauce, onion flakes, onion powder, Italian seasoning, garlic powder, salt, and pepper in a deep cast iron pan.

2 Mix well to create a sauce, then simmer over indirect heat.

3 Grill the bacon.

4 Combine the ground pork, beef, SPG seasoning, and diced onion, and form into meatballs.

5 Grill the meatballs over direct heat to sear the outside before placing them into the sauce mix. Cover and let flavors combine.

6 Place the meatballs and sauce into bread rolls, then top with cheese and bacon. Place back on the grill to melt the cheese.

7 Serve hot.

SCAN & WATCH

It's real easy to do!

GUINNESS MEATBALLS

INGREDIENTS

- 2 lb ground beef
- 6 oz Guinness beer

These quick and easy two-ingredient Guinness meatballs are perfect for any tailgate.

METHOD

1 Add 6 oz of Guinness to the ground beef and mix well. No other seasoning required.

2 Make the meatballs and place them away from the coals over indirect heat. Close the lid of the grill.

3 Rotate and flip the meatballs halfway through cooking to get an even cook. Cook until the meatballs reach an internal temperature of 160°F, about 30 minutes.

4 Remove and serve as snacks, or as a main meal, with your choice of sides.

PITMASTER PRIVILEGE

Serve these with a few of your favorite rubs, seasonings, sides, and dipping sauces.

We're cooking up a storm out here!

CAJUN JAMBALAYA

INGREDIENTS (+ MARINADE)

- 1 lb chicken thighs, boneless and skinless
- 1 lb andouille sausage
- 2 sticks of celery, diced
- 1 onion, diced
- 1 bell pepper, green or red, diced
- 8 cloves garlic, crushed
- 2 tbsp salt
- SPG seasoning
- 1 tsp fresh ground black pepper
- 1 fresh chili pepper, diced (we used tabasco chili), choose your favorite
- 6 cups of chicken stock
- 2 cups of rice, use long grain
- 3 tbsp butter
- 3 green onions, thinly sliced
- ½ cup canola oil or any high smoke point cooking oil
- ½ cup all-purpose flour

This dish, a southern staple of a Louisiana kitchen, won't let you down. Getting the roux right can be tricky, but follow the instructions and you'll get a Cajun jambalaya right the first time.

METHOD (THE CHICKEN)

1 Season the chicken all over with SPG seasoning.

2 Sear the chicken on both sides until browned all over.

THE ROUX

3 Heat ½ cup of oil in the saucepan.

4 Add ½ cup of flour and stir constantly over medium heat until the roux turns a chocolate brown color.

5 DO NOT stop stirring it; if the roux burns even slightly, it will be ruined.

COOKING

6 Add the diced celery, bell pepper, onion, salt, and pepper, and mix well into the roux.

7 Add the crushed garlic and chili pepper.

8 Add the chicken stock and simmer over medium-low heat for about 1 hour.

9 Add in the sausage, chicken, and rice, and cover to cook for a further 30 minutes until the rice is cooked.

10 Stir in the butter and top with green onions and (optionally) fresh chopped chilis.

11 Serve hot.

SCAN & WATCH

Man, you gotta try this out!

BBQ BACON MEATBALL STUFFED ONION

INGREDIENTS

- 1 lb bacon, regular cut
- 2 lb ground chuck
- 6 large sweet onions, cored, leftovers reserved
- SPG seasoning, to taste
- 2 tbsp BBQ sauce
- 2 tbsp mozzarella cheese, grated
- 2 pickled jalapeños, sliced

Or call them grilled meatballs topped with cheese and wrapped in bacon and onions if ya want. Nonetheless, they're good eating at the Pit!

METHOD

1 Preheat grill.

2 Add some of the reserved onion leftovers to the ground chuck, season, and mix well.

3 Form the meat into balls, then stuff them inside the cored onions.

4 Wrap the onions with bacon slices.

5 Place the onions on the grill over indirect heat, cover, and cook at 250°F–275°F for about 2 hours.

6 When the onions are just about done, brush them with barbecue sauce. Grill for another 10 minutes.

7 Top the onions with cheese and pickled jalapeño slices, then grill until the cheese is melted.

8 Serve with your choice of dip.

BBQ PIT BOYS

BEEF 'N' BACON MOZZARELLA BALLS

INGREDIENTS

- ¾ lb ground beef chuck
- ¼ lb ground pork
- thin sliced pork belly bacon
- chili relish or use you favorite relish or pickle
- fresh mozzarella, sliced
- pickled jalapeño slices
- SPG seasoning, or your favorite
- toothpicks

Packed with fresh mozzarella, jalapeños, and chili relish and topped with melted mozzarella, these beef 'n' bacon balls are quick & easy to do!

METHOD

1 Season with SPG and mix together the ground pork and beef and form into patties.

2 Spread some chili relish onto each patty. Top with a good amount of mozzarella and a few sliced jalapeños.

3 Form each patty into a ball, making sure you seal off as much as possible so the melting cheese doesn't leak out.

4 Wrap each ball with two rounds of pork belly bacon, securing each ball with a toothpick.

5 Place the bacon-wrapped balls opposite the hot coals at a temperature around 350°F.

6 At about the halfway point, as the bacon begins to tighten and brown, rotate for even cooking. At this point you can add a few pieces for your favorite smoke wood.

7 Check that the internal temperature is close to 165°F, then top each of the balls with a slice of the fresh mozzarella. Once the cheese is melted, remove from the grill & serve hot.

Ohhhhh, sweet Martha!

SCAN &
WATCH

SCAN & WATCH

FIREBALL WHISKEY MEATBALLS

INGREDIENTS

- 3 lb ground chuck, 80/20 (meat/fat)
- 1 lb pork belly bacon, regular sliced
- SPG seasoning, to taste
- 2 cups cinnamon-flavored whiskey

These atomic fireball meatballs are quick and easy to grill up at the Pit. If you don't like (or don't have) cinnamon whiskey, use your favorite brand of whiskey or bourbon.

METHOD

1 Bring grill temperature up to 300°F, with coals offset for indirect cooking.

2 In a bowl, season the ground chuck to taste and add 1–2 shots (1½–3 oz) cinnamon flavored whiskey.

3 Mix well.

4 Hand form meatballs, 4–6 oz. each. This should yield 7–9 meatballs.

5 Wrap each meatball with sliced bacon, approximately two pieces per meatball.

6 Place meatballs opposite hot coals for indirect cooking. Place lid on grill. Maintain 300°F.

7 After 30 minutes, rotate meatballs for even cooking. Inject each meatball with a shot of cinnamon whiskey (½ to 1 oz each).

8 Cover grill and cook for an additional 20 minutes.

9 Transfer meatballs to a serving tray and let sit for a couple of minutes.

10 Sit back, relax, and enjoy!

You know how to do that!

BEEF

WHETHER IT'S STEAK 'N' BACON SCALLOPS COOKED OVER AN OPEN FIRE IN THE WILDERNESS, OR GRILLED BEEF TENDERLOIN STEAK STUFFED WITH LOBSTER AND COVERED WITH A WHISKEY PEPPERCORN SAUCE, THIS NEXT CHUNK OF RECIPES ALL HAVE ONE THING IN COMMON: THEY SURE TASTE GUUUD... SWEET MARTHA!

SCAN & WATCH

Guuud livin' don't get any better than this!

STEAK 'N' BACON SCALLOP SUB

INGREDIENTS

FOR THE BURGER

- 1 steak, thick cut
- 6 fresh sea scallops
- 1 lb ground beef
- 2 green onions
- ¼–½ lb cheese, sliced
- fresh bacon
- 1 tbsp SPG seasoning
- 1 tsp maple sugar rub
- ¼–½ lb butter
- sub-style buns
- fresh cucumber, sliced

PITMASTER PRIVILEGE

You can use any rub or seasoning you like but you gotta check this out—this is GUUUD!

Cooked over an open fire in the wilderness, this steak 'n' bacon scallop sub is a work of art wrapped in bread. With just a grill grate and few sticks of wood, Pitmaster Handzee knocks this sandwich up and out of the park. It's real easy to do and it's GUUUD!

METHOD

1 Set up your grill for indirect cooking.

2 Take a bacon strip and wrap it around a sea scallop, then skewer it. Complete this process until you have all of the scallops skewered on the stick. Cook on the grill over medium heat, then move off the coals when done.

3 Divide the ground beef into two patties.

4 Sprinkle SPG seasoning and maple sugar rub all over the patties and gently rub into both sides. Do the same with the steak.

5 Smear a generous pat of butter onto one side of the steak. Place the steak and the two patties over the coals to sear. Add a small pat of butter to the patties while on the grill.

6 Sear the edges of the steak if desired. When done, move the steak off the coals to continue cooking indirectly. Move the patties away from the coals as well.

7 Sear the green onions, then chop them up. Thinly slice the seared steaks.

8 Top the patties with cheese and green onions, then place them in a cast iron pan on the grill. Add a little water to the pan, close the lid, and cook for a minute or so to melt the cheese.

9 Toast the buns a little.

10 Butter a toasted bun, add some sliced cucumber, the beef patties, grilled bacon scallops, and a few slices of grilled steak, and you have a tasty steak 'n' bacon scallop sub!

STEAK & OYSTERS SEAFOOD

INGREDIENTS

- 2 steaks (your favorite kind), 1½ inch thick, trimmed of excess fat
- fresh-shucked oysters
- SPG seasoning
- 2 tbsp butter
- 6 oz dark beer
- ¼ cup brown sugar
- 1 tbsp Worcestershire sauce
- french fries for serving
- skewers

This 100-year-old recipe was a favorite steak dinner of the nouveau riche in the northern states during the industrial revolution. And for good reason! That grilled beef steak stuffed with fresh-shucked oyster flavor is real tasty and a surf and turf classic.

METHOD

1 Set up your grill for indirect grilling. Place hot coals on one side of the grill and no coals on the other side of the grill.

2 Cut a pocket into each steak by making a slit in the side, stuff the pocket with oysters, and seal it with skewers.

3 Season the steaks on both sides with SPG seasoning.

4 Place a small pot on the grill over the hot coals and add the beer, brown sugar, some SPG, and 1 tbsp of butter. Stir and move to the side of the grill with no coals.

5 Let simmer for a few minutes, then add the Worcestershire sauce—taste and add more SPG if needed. Remove from the grill and set aside.

6 Place the steaks on the grill directly over the hot coals and sear for 2 minutes each side.

7 When seared, move the steaks to the side of the grill with no coals to finish cooking and cover the grill with the lid. Cook the steaks to your desired doneness.

8 When steaks are done, place a skillet on the grill directly over the hot coals. Add 1 tbsp of butter to the skillet to melt.

9 Add any extra oysters to the skillet and fry in the butter.

10 Place a steak on top of a bed of french fries.

11 Place the fried oysters on top of the steak, top everything with the steak sauce, serve, and enjoy!

SCAN & WATCH

You're talkin' the ultimate surf 'n' turf right here...

Martha's gonna love this!

LOBSTER-STUFFED FILET MIGNON STEAK

INGREDIENTS

- 2 lb lobster, steamed
- 4 lb beef tenderloin steaks
- olive oil
- 2 tbsp green onion, minced
- 2 tbsp garlic, minced
- 2 tbsp celery, minced
- 4 cups breadcrumbs
- 4 slices bacon, smoked
- hot sauce, to taste
- butter
- water
- salt and pepper, to taste
- toothpick

WHISKEY PEPPERCORN SAUCE

- 1 cup beef broth
- 2 tbsp fresh ground pepper
- 1 cup heavy cream
- one shot or more of your favorite whiskey
- salt

For a special holiday, try this grilled beef tenderloin steak, stuffed with lobster and covered with a whiskey peppercorn sauce.

METHOD

1 Rub the beef tenderloin with salt, pepper, and olive oil.

2 Make pockets in the beef filets with a knife.

3 Take the meat out of the lobster tail, and chop into large chunks.

4 Add the butter to a pan and sauté green onion, celery, and minced garlic.

5 Tip in the breadcrumbs and cook further.

6 Add a little water and hot sauce to bind it out, stir well.

7 Add the lobster chunks and heat a little.

8 Take the pan off the heat and set aside.

9 In another pot, mix the beef broth and fresh ground pepper and heat to reduce.

10 Season the broth with salt.

11 Add the whiskey and heavy cream, reduce the liquid, and set aside when done.

12 Fill each beef filet pocket with about a tablespoon of the lobster meat.

13 Fasten each opening with a slice of bacon and secure with a toothpick.

14 Repeat with the other steaks.

15 Place the steaks onto the grill over the coals.

16 Cook for a minute or two on each side to sear.

17 Place on indirect heat and cover the grill for about 40 minutes until the meat is cooked.

18 Once the meat is cooked, take it off the grill.

19 Serve the filet mignons with the whiskey sauce.

BBQ PIT BOYS

This is some
guuud eatin'!

RIB STEAKS & SCALLOPS WITH CLAM SAUCE

INGREDIENTS

- 2 lb rib steak, 2-inch thick
- SPG seasoning
- 10–12 sea scallops
- 1 lb clams in shell
- 1 garlic clove, crushed
- 2 tbsp shallot, finely diced
- 2 tbsp lemon juice
- 1 stick butter
- Old Bay seasoning
- 1 cup chopped clams
- 1 cup white wine
- ½–¾ cup heavy cream
- salt

Get that raise or promotion you wanted from your boss, or better yet, hook up with that new girly you met? You just found the recipe to celebrate with!

METHOD

1 Set up two grills for indirect heat (hot coals on one side of the grill and no coals on the other side of the grill).

2 Season both sides of the steak with SPG or your favorite seasoning and place directly over the hot coals to sear. Each side needs about 3–4 minutes.

3 Place a skillet over the coals on the second grill to heat up.

4 Lightly season the scallops on one side only, with salt and Old Bay seasoning. Do not over-season.

5 Melt 1 tbsp of butter in the skillet. Add the shallots and garlic and leave to sweat for a couple of minutes. Then add the white wine, a little more butter, and the lemon juice.

6 Finally, add the clams, cover the grill with the lid, and steam until the clams have opened up.

7 Once the steak has been seared on both sides, move it away from the coals, and cover the grill with the lid. Rotate the steak once during cooking.

8 Add the heavy cream and chopped clams to the shallot and garlic pan, move off the coals, and cover the grill so the sauce can reduce.

9 Place a second skillet over the coals—it needs to be very hot to sear the scallops. Melt 2 tbsp of butter in the skillet and, when hot, add the scallops. Sear for 2 minutes each side or until brown. Do not overcook.

10 When the steak is cooked, remove from the grill and allow to rest a couple of minutes so the juices redistribute throughout the meat.

11 Place the steak, scallops, and clams on a plate, then pour the clam sauce over the top. Serve and enjoy!

TRI-TIP STEAKS

INGREDIENTS

- 2 tri-tip steaks
- BBQ seasoning
- 1 tbsp olive oil
- hard wood chunks—fruity wood like pecan—soaked in water
- for potato bombs recipe, see page 89

PITMASTER PRIVILEGE

You can use any rub you like for this steak. Find a selection on our website—or for SPG, use garlic, salt, and pepper; for Sweet Martha, use equal parts sugar, paprika, and mustard powder.

Tri-tips are real popular for grilling, and for good reason. They're cut from the beef sirloin and are full of that rich beef flavor that steak masters demand when serving up that special steak to friends and family. Serve them up with some BBQ Pit Boys potato bombs and now you're talking good eatin' at the Pit!

METHOD

1 Set up your grill for indirect heat (hot coals on one side of the grill and no coals on the other side)—You're looking for a temp between 250°F–275°F.

2 Lightly oil steaks on both sides, then liberally coat with BBQ seasoning. Leave to set for 45 minutes to one hour.

3 Soak your hardwood chunks in water. This allows the wood to smoke and not burn up right away.

4 If you're serving this steak dish with potato bombs (see page 89) now put the potatoes on the grill, opposite the coals.

5 After about 45 minutes, place your steaks on the side of the grill with no coals. Add a piece of soaked hardwood onto the hot coals.

6 Cook time will be about 2 hours, depending on your grill temperature. After 1 hour, rotate the steaks 180 degrees to help them cook evenly, and add another chunk of hardwood to the coals.

7 After 1 hour 15 minutes, check internal temperature of the steaks with an instant read thermometer. When they are at 130 degrees, place them directly over hot coals to sear—about 2 minutes per side. Move the potatoes to indirect heat.

8 Take steaks off the grill and let them rest for 10 minutes to let the juices redistribute throughout the meat.

9 Slice the steak thinly across the grain of the steak.

10. Plate the steak and add a potato bomb—and enjoy!

Real popular for grilling, and with good reason!

SCAN & WATCH

Ooooh Baby—that smells GUUUD!

STRIP STEAK & WHISKEY GRAVY

INGREDIENTS

- 2 x 1½ inch thick New York strip steaks
- SPG seasoning
- 2 celery stalks, chopped
- 1 onion, chopped
- 2 garlic cloves, chopped
- ¼ cup cooking oil
- 4 tbsp unsalted butter
- 4 tbsp flour
- ½ cup whiskey
- 2 cups beef stock
- salt and pepper, to taste

Whiskey gravy tastes real good on most anything, but especially on these New York strip steaks. So dig out your grill and fire it up!

METHOD

1 Set up your grill for indirect cooking at 450°F.

2 Place the pot over the hot coals and add the cooking oil, then add the celery and onion to sauté. Cook until they are caramelized.

3 Add the garlic to the pot just before the onions are caramelized. You do not want to burn the garlic.

4 Remove the vegetables from the pot and set aside. Move the pot with the remaining oil off the coals.

5 Add the butter to the pot to melt, then gradually add the flour, stirring as it's added. Cook until it is slightly brown, then add the whiskey and beef stock.

6 Stir well, scraping the bottom of the pot to loosen any bits stuck there—this adds a lot of flavor to the gravy.

7 Add your onions, celery, and garlic back into the pot, and season with salt and pepper to taste.

8 The gravy will need to simmer for 20 to 30 minutes to thicken. Stir occasionally.

9 After about 15 minutes liberally season both sides of the steak with the SPG (or your favorite seasoning), and place the steaks directly over the hot coals to sear.

10 Sear each side for 2–3 minutes, to finish cooking move them to the side of the grill with no coals and cover the grill.

11 When cooked as desired, take the steaks off the grill and let rest to redistribute the juices throughout the meat.

12 When they're ready, put the steaks on a plate and ladle the gravy and vegetables over the top.

13 Serve with crusty fresh bread and enjoy!

SCAN & WATCH

I say it's time to eat!

SCAN &

WATCH

BBQ PIT BOYS

BBQ PIT BOYS

BBQ PIT BOYS

SCAN &
WATCH

LONDON BROIL GRILLED STEAK

INGREDIENTS

- 6 lb round steak, trimmed of excess fat and cut into 4 steaks
- 2 large resealable plastic bags

FOR THE MARINADE

- 12–16 oz beer
- ½ cup olive oil
- 1 tsp cayenne pepper
- 1 tbsp garlic powder
- 1 tbsp onion powder
- 2 tbsp Worcestershire sauce
- 1 tbsp ground pepper
- 1 tbsp prepared horseradish
- juice of ½ lemon

The round steak, sometimes referred to as a topside and silverside, can be a tough cut of beef steak unless you first marinate it for a few hours.

METHOD

1 In a bowl, mix all the marinade ingredients.

2 Place two steaks in each resealable plastic bag.

3 Pour ⅓ of the marinade into each bag—seal and knead the bags to cover each steak.

4 Place the steak in a refrigerator for between 4 to 24 hours.

5 Set the grill up for direct cooking—you want a medium heat.

6 Place steaks directly over the hot coals. Depending on the thickness of the steak, each side will need about 8 minutes.

7 Cook to your desired doneness. You can check this by placing an instant read thermometer into the side of the steak towards the center.

8 Let the steak rest for 5 minutes to allow the juices to redistribute throughout the meat.

9 Cut the steak into thin slices across the grain.

10 Serve and enjoy!

It sure tastes GUUUUUD!!

TOP SIRLOIN BEEF ROAST

INGREDIENTS

- **9 lb top sirloin, halved**
- **¼ cup beef rub (chipotle or any kind), as needed**
- **condiments for serving**

Many prize this cut of beef, cut from under the tenderloin, because of its intense beefy flavor. Also known as a spoon roast in the states, the Pit Boys use the "double rub" technique and cook it slow and indirect over medium heat to produce a tender and juicy beef roast second to none. And it's real easy to do with these few simple tips.

METHOD

1 Coat the meat pieces generously with the rub and wrap them with plastic wrap. Set aside for 4 hours or overnight.

2 Preheat the grill to a medium temperature of 250°F–275°F.

3 Place sirloin pieces on the grill, over indirect heat, cover, and cook for about 30 minutes. Turn the meat pieces and continue to cook.

4 After 75 minutes (or when the internal temperature reaches 100°F) remove the meat pieces from the grill and wipe them lightly to remove excess moisture.

5 Coat them again with the rub and place back on the grill, over direct flame. Cover and cook until done, flipping them every 5 minutes during this time for even cooking.

6 Wrap the meat with foil and set aside for 10–15 minutes to rest.

7 Carve the roast and serve on a bun or in a sandwich with your favorite condiments.

You've definitely got to check this out... MAN it's guuuud.

SCAN &
WATCH

BBQ PIT BOYS

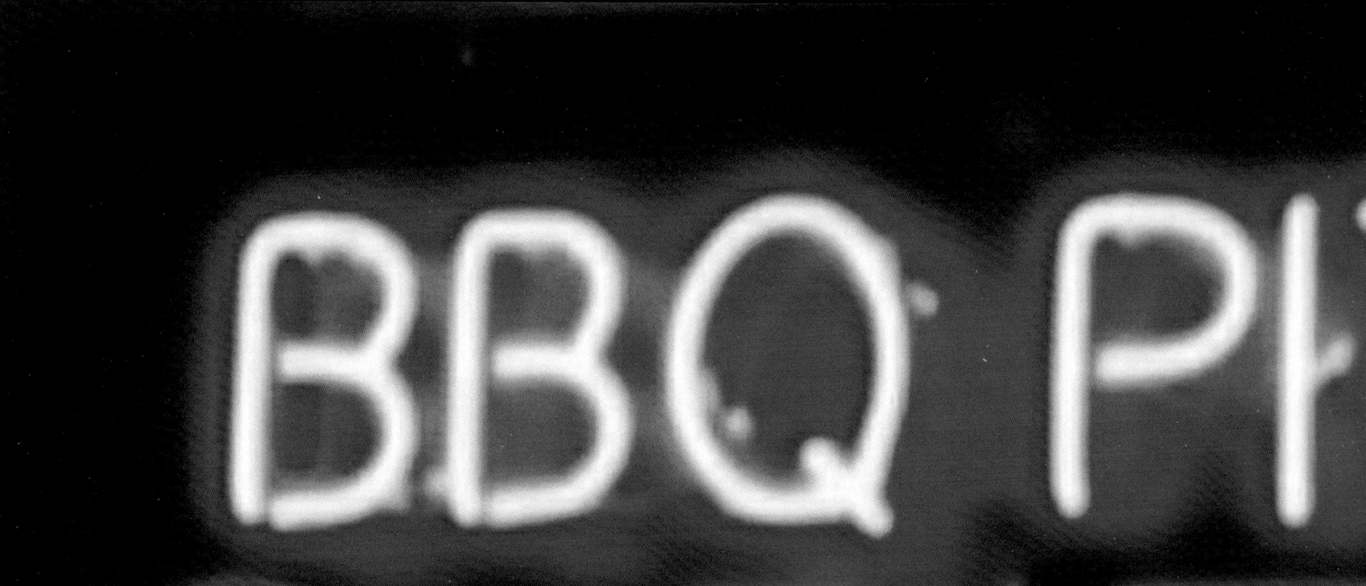

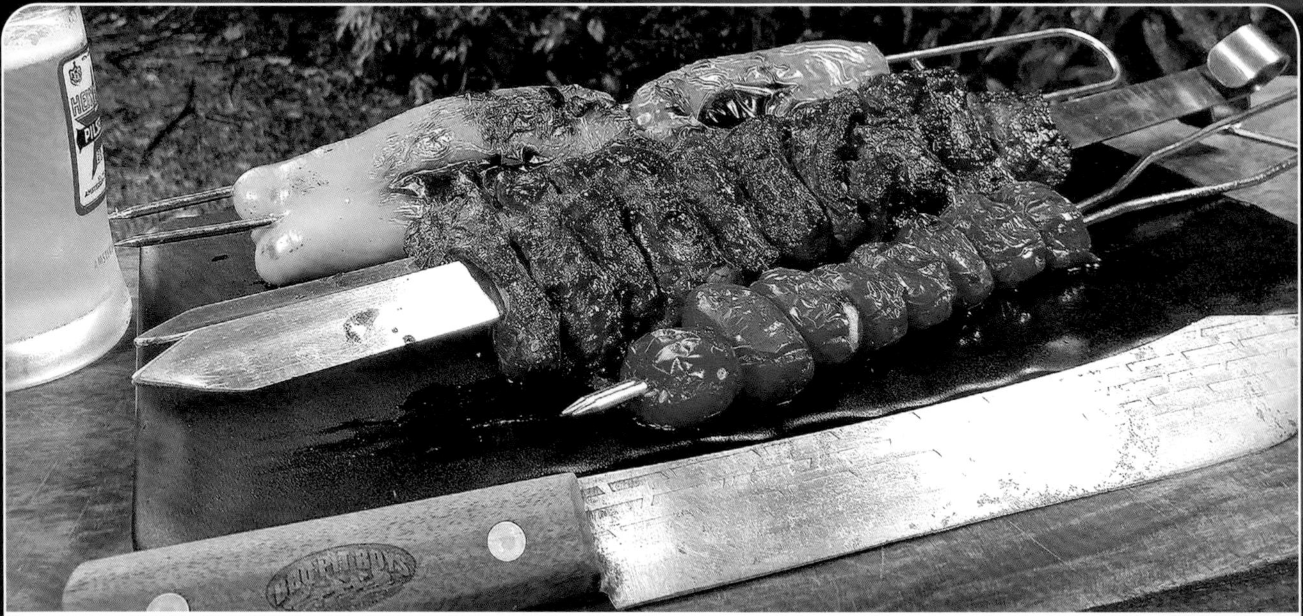

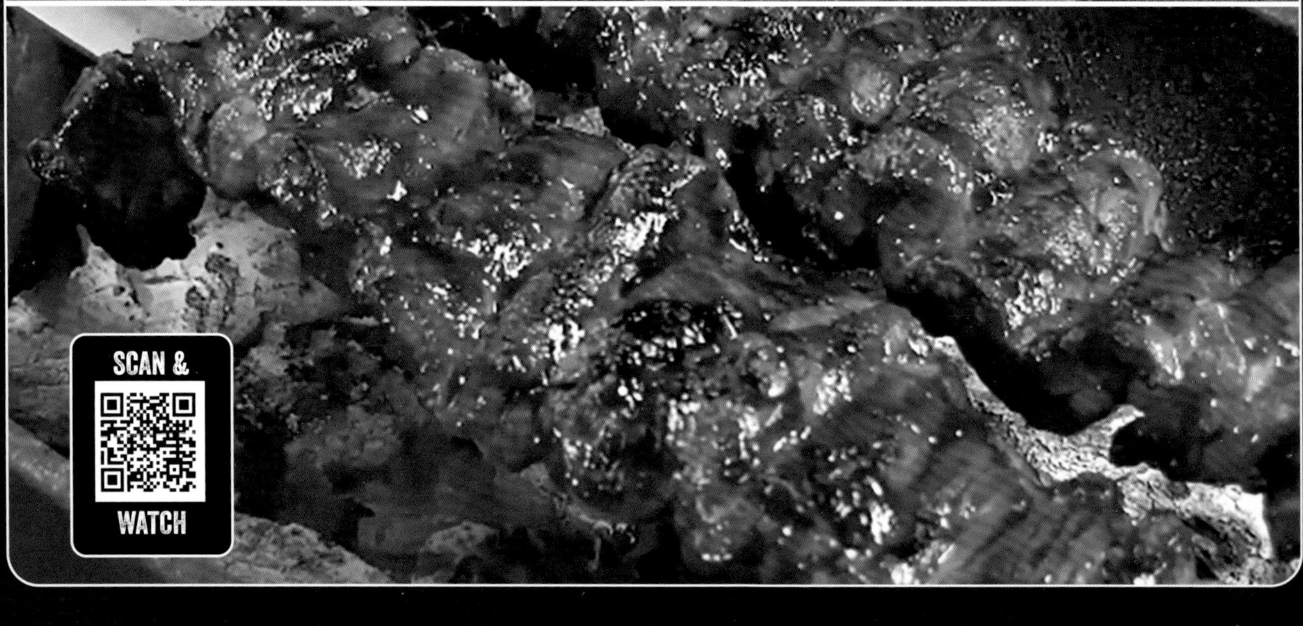

SCAN &

WATCH

BEEF 'N' WHISKEY KEBABS

INGREDIENTS

- 4 lb beef tenderloin
- 2 green bell peppers
- 2 cups cherry tomatoes
- 1 cup bourbon whiskey, ½ at start of reduction, ½ at end
- ½ cup brown sugar
- 1 cup ketchup
- 3 tbsp red chili flakes
- 1 tbsp white pepper
- ½ tsp SPG seasoning
- 2 tsp Worcestershire sauce
- 2 green onion stems, chopped

With this real simple bourbon sauce recipe and a few slices of beef tenderloin served with grilled tomatoes and grilled bell peppers, these beef 'n' bourbon kebabs will blow your mind.

METHOD

1 To a small bowl, add ½ cup whiskey, red chili flakes, white pepper, soy sauce, brown sugar, ketchup, and garlic.

2 Roughly chop the green onions, add to the bowl, and mix.

3 Add the mix to a pot and heat to thicken. Add SPG seasoning and hot sauce if desired.

4 Core, de-seed, and skewer the peppers. Skewer the cherry tomatoes separately.

5 Halve the tenderloin, then butterfly each half into a single large, thin slice. Halve each slice vertically.

6 Thread each piece of sliced tenderloin onto a flat skewer—this prevents the meat from spinning while cooking.

7 Place the tenderloin skewers over direct heat and brush liberally with sauce. Flip, brush the other side with sauce, and continue turning the skewers occasionally as they cook.

8 Cook the vegetable skewers over direct heat, turning occasionally as needed. The vegetable skewers will have a shorter cook time; you can grill them separately or add them to the grill after the meat has had some time to cook.

9 Serve and enjoy!

TERIYAKI BEEF TENDERLOIN

INGREDIENTS

- 3 lb beef tenderloin—
  6 steaks
- coarse salt and pepper or
  SPG seasoning

FOR THE SAUCE

- 1 cup soy sauce
- 2 cup sake
- ¾ cup sugar
- 2 tbsp malt vinegar
- 4 tbsp black pepper
- 6 garlic cloves, smashed and peeled
- 6 green onions, roughly chopped

Step up that mild flavor of beef tenderloin with teriyaki sauce for the best beef tenderloin experience you've ever had with these samurai beef steaks.

METHOD

1 Generously season beef steaks with salt and pepper or your favorite seasonings.

2 Chop up the garlic and green onions.

3 To a preheated pan, add sake, soy sauce, vinegar, pepper, sugar, and mix. Add the chopped garlic and green onions, and simmer to thicken.

4 Place skewered beef over direct coals.

5 Keep turning the steaks regularly, basting the steaks with the sauce every time.

6 Cook until the internal temperature reaches about 125°F, then remove steaks to rest before cutting into them.

7 You can add some chilis for heat, or adjust the soy and sugar quantities according to your taste preference.

BBQ PIT BOYS

SCAN & WATCH

BBQ PIT BOYS

This is some guuud eatin'!

OXTAIL BEEF 'N' BEER STEW

INGREDIENTS

- 5 lb oxtail (beef tails)
- 1 cup chopped onions
- 8–10 cups beef broth
- 6 carrots, sliced
- 4 stalks celery
- 2 bay leaves
- 4 sprigs parsley
- 4 cups diced potatoes
- 24 oz beer
- salt and pepper, to taste
- vegetable oil

Check out this BBQ Pit Boys beef and beer stew that will get ya through the day, no matter what Old Man Winter is throwin' at ya.

METHOD

1 Sauté the chopped onions.

2 Coat the oxtails with oil, then season with salt and pepper.

3 Sear all sides of the oxtails over open flame, then add to a pot.

4 Add 8 cups beef broth to the pot.

5 Add 24 oz beer to the pot.

6 Add bay leaves to the pot.

7 Add parsley sprigs to the pot.

8 Cook at a slow simmer for 6 hours or until beef falls off the bone. Add more beef broth if necessary to keep the oxtails submerged.

9 When the oxtails are done, remove from the pot and debone. Add carrots and celery. Simmer for 10 minutes, then add potatoes.

10 Simmer until potatoes are tender. Add oxtails to pot.

11 Serve and enjoy!

OTHER MEATS: PORK, LAMB & GAME

ST. LOUIS STYLE, BUTTERSCOTCH BOURBON STYLE, MARGARITA OR GRILLED ASIAN STYLE, THIS HERE CHAPTER IS STUFFED FULL OF ONE OF MARTHA'S FAVORITES—RIBS! BUT THERE'S PLENTY OF OTHER OPTIONS TOO: GRILLED BACON RIBBITS, PIT BOYS PORK AND BEANS, OR IF YOU'RE FEELING ADVENTUROUS, ALLIGATOR TENDERLOIN. WHATEVER YOU CHOOSE, IT'S ALL GOOD EATING DOWN AT THE PIT!

Man, oh man, that smells Guuud...

BUTTERSCOTCH BOURBON RIBS

INGREDIENTS

- 2 racks pork ribs
- 2 cups butterscotch bits
- ½ stick butter
- ¼ stick butter
- ½ cup brown sugar
- 2 tbsp garlic, minced
- ½ cup cider vinegar
- 1 cup onions, diced
- 1 cup bourbon
- 1 tsp cayenne pepper
- olive oil
- SPG seasoning

That's right, butterscotch bourbon ribs! Some call these sweet pork candy, and you'll see why with that first bite.

METHOD

1 Remove the membrane from both racks of ribs.

2 Coat the ribs with olive oil and SPG seasoning.

3 Get some hot coals going on your grill on one side, leaving the cool side open. Bring the temperature up to 275°F–300°F and place both racks opposite the hot coals. Place one small piece of applewood on the hot coals for some added smoke.

4 In a sauce pan over low heat, melt ½ stick of butter.

5 As soon as the butter is almost all melted, pour in the butterscotch bits, stirring quickly to avoid letting the butterscotch burn. Then pour in the cider vinegar, still stirring constantly. Stir continuously until smooth. Do not let burn.

6 Pour in the brown sugar, the cayenne pepper, and the minced garlic, and keep stirring until smooth. Once fully mixed, set aside.

7 In a frying pan, melt ¼ stick of butter with a splash of olive oil and start caramelizing the diced onions.

8 Put the butterscotch back on very low heat and pour in the caramelized onions and the bourbon, stirring until all ingredients are mixed.

9 Halfway through the cook, slather the butterscotch mix onto the ribs. Brush the ribs with sauce about three or four more times until the meat has pulled in, exposing the bones, and the meat is tender.

10 Serve and enjoy!

MARGARITA RIBS

INGREDIENTS

- 6 lb of pork spare ribs—we had our butcher saw the racks in half
- 12 oz can beer

FOR THE MARGARITA BRINE

- 1 cup water
- 1 cup tequila
- juice of 2 limes
- 4 tbsp triple sec liqueur
- 4 tbsp coarse salt
- 2 tbsp sugar
- 1 tbsp cayenne pepper
- 1 tbsp orange zest

FOR THE RUB

- ½ cup paprika
- ¼ cup black pepper
- 2 tbsp garlic powder
- 2 tbsp onion powder
- 1 tbsp cayenne pepper
- ½ cup chili powder
- ½ cup of coarse salt
- ½ cup brown sugar

Grilled half-cut pork spare ribs, marinated in a Tequila, lime, and Triple Sec brine, makes what we Pit Boys call Margarita Ribs.

METHOD

1 Place the ribs in a large plastic bag with water, tequila, triple sec, coarse salt, lime juice, sugar, orange zest, and cayenne pepper.

2 Seal the bag, kneading and turning it to mix all the ingredients evenly, and marinate in the fridge for 2 hours.

3 Mix all the rub ingredients together. Once the ribs have finished marinating, coat them in the rub.

4 Set up your grill for indirect cooking at about 300°F. Add a pan of water under the grill on the side without coals to add moisture while cooking.

5 Lay the ribs close together on the grill over indirect heat, over the pan of water. Cover the grill and cook for about 45 minutes.

6 Rotate the ribs on the grill for an even cook, then brush the tops with beer. Re-cover and cook for another hour and a half.

7 After roughly two hours, uncover the grill to brush the ribs with your favorite tomato-based sauce. Cover again, cook for another 30 minutes, and flip the ribs to brush the other side with sauce.

8 Cover the grill and cook for roughly 20 more minutes.

9 Remove the ribs from the grill, serve with your favorite sides, and enjoy.

There ain't gonna be any leftovers!

ASIAN GRILLED BARBEQUE RIBS

INGREDIENTS

- 2 slabs pork spare ribs—
  3 lb each, trimmed
  St. Louis style

FOR THE MARINADE

- ½ cup hoisin sauce
- ½ cup oyster sauce
- ½ cup soy sauce
- 4 tbsp minced garlic
- ½–1 tsp cayenne pepper

FOR THE MOPPING/BASTING SAUCE

- 3 tbsp soy sauce
- 1 tsp honey

This is a real easy-to-make classic Asian dish. Cook it real slow, and keep mopping with sauce, and you won't regret it! Man alive, it's guuud!

METHOD

1 Bring grill temperature up to 275°F, with coals offset for indirect cooking.

2 Thoroughly combine marinade in a bowl and set aside.

3 Mix mopping/basting sauce thoroughly and set aside.

4 Cut up ribs into individual, single bone sections.

5 Place rib cutlets into bowl of marinade. Using your hands, coat ribs with marinade. Place ribs in the refrigerator for 2–3 hours, no longer.

6 Place ribs opposite hot coals in a single layer for indirect cooking. Cover grill and cook for 30 minutes.

7 Remove lid and mop with mopping/basting sauce. Turn and rotate ribs for even cooking. Cover and cook another 30 minutes.

8 Remove lid and baste again. Turn and rotate ribs for even cooking. Cover grill and cook for another 30 minutes.

9 Continue basting and turning/rotating ribs every 30 minutes for a total cook time of 3 hours.

10 Remove ribs from grill and place on a platter with dipping sauce.

11 Serve with a side of fried rice, salad, ginger mashed potatoes, or just by themselves.

12 Sit back, relax, and enjoy!

And by the miracle of time, I give to you a taste sensation!

SCAN &
WATCH

Take a look at that! Perfect!

ST. LOUIS SPARE RIBS

INGREDIENTS

- 4–5 lb pork back spare ribs
- 1–2 tbsp olive oil
- your favorite dry rub or seasoning
- 1 bottle St. Louis sauce, or your favorite BBQ sauce, for basting and serving

PITMASTER PRIVILEGE

Use any dry rub, BBQ sauce, or seasoning mix you want for these ribs.

Here we show you how to trim up and then barbecue, "low and slow," some great-tasting St. Louis style BBQ spare ribs. It doesn't get much better than this!

METHOD

1 To start, choose some fresh pork spare ribs.

2 Preheat your grill to 225°F–250°F.

3 Wash and dry the ribs.

4 Trim any excess fat and remove the membrane.

5 Rub a little olive oil over the ribs and then apply the dry rub or seasoning of your choice to both sides of the slab. Let it stand for 15–30 minutes.

6 Allow the ribs to come to room temperature just before placing on the grill.

7 Place a water or basting pan on the grill, or within the coals for added moisture (optional but recommended).

8 Close the lid and grill at 225°F–250°F opposite the coals for about 4 hours.

9 During cooking, mop/baste the ribs several times with St. Louis sauce or your favorite BBQ sauce.

10 When they pull apart easily, with meat still attached to the bone, remove the racks from the grill. They are DONE!

11 Cut them up and serve with your favorite barbecue sauce and enjoy!

VARIATION – STANDING ST. LOUIS RIBS

1 After step 4 above, roll the ribs into a round and tie with string twice around the "stand" of ribs to hold it together.

2 Rub a little olive oil over the ribs and then pat onto the moist meat the dry rub or seasoning of your choice.

3 Stand the ribs in a cast iron pan with 1–2 cups of stock in the bottom. Optionally, add a roughly chopped onion to the pan. Continue from step 7 above.

GRILLED BACON RIBBITS

INGREDIENTS

- 4 frogs, cleaned
- 1 orange, cut into quarters
- 8 chilies
- 8 slices bacon

FOR THE BASTING SAUCE

- 4 tbsp butter
- 1 tbsp ground black pepper
- 4 thin slices ginger
- 1 shallot, minced
- pickled peppers—to taste

All that croakin' noise at night gettin' to ya? A few grilled bacon wrapped bull frogs and some ice cold Buds will keep the mud pond quiet. A New Orleans Cajun tribute to Justin Wilson, "I gar-on-tee!"

METHOD

1 Set up your grill for direct grilling—medium heat.

2 Place ¼ of an orange into the body cavity of each frog.

3 Wrap each frog in 2 slices of bacon.

4 Place 2 chilies into the mouth of each frog.

MAKING THE BASTING SAUCE

5 Place the skillet on the grill and add the butter, black pepper, ginger, minced shallot, and pickled peppers, to taste.

COOKING

6 Place the frogs directly over the coals.

7 Continually baste until done cooking.

8 Frogs are done when the bacon is cooked.

9 Serve and Enjoy!

SCAN & WATCH

PIT BOYS PORK & BEANS

INGREDIENTS

- 1 tbsp vegetable oil (as needed)
- 1 bacon slab, cut into 1-inch pieces
- 90 oz canned white beans
- 1 onion, finely chopped
- 4 cups ketchup
- ½ cup brown sugar
- ¼ cup molasses
- 2 tbsp dry mustard
- 4 tbsp vinegar
- salt and pepper, to taste

Hold off on the baked beans because we're cooking up some old-school style pork and beans.

METHOD

1 Preheat grill.

2 Place a large pot over direct flame of grill and pour oil in it. Add bacon and fry for a couple of minutes.

3 Add onion, sauté, and then add beans, ketchup, brown sugar, molasses, dry mustard, vinegar, salt, and pepper. Give it a good stir.

4 Place pot over indirect heat, cover and simmer for 2–3 hours or until done. Stir midway and rotate pot.

5 Remove from grill and let sit before serving.

6 Serve hot and enjoy with grilled sausage and bread.

SCAN & WATCH

WHISKEY-GLAZED SMOKED HAM

INGREDIENTS

FOR THE GLAZE

- 3 serrano chilies, finely diced
- ¼ cup whiskey
- 1¼ cup apricot or orange marmalade
- ¼ cup molasses
- 3 tbsp soy sauce
- 2 tbsp brown sugar

FOR THE HAM

- approx. 16 lb wet-cured ham
- pork rub—your favorite
- 1 can pineapple rings
- toothpicks
- apple juice (you can substitute with water or beer)

Man, I'm hungry!

This whole ham done on the grill is as good as it gets. Learn how easy it is to make a tender and moist "all holiday" whiskey-glazed smoked ham for your next special occasion barbeque.

METHOD

1 Set up your grill for indirect heat (hot coals on one side of the grill and no coals on the other side of the grill). You're looking for a temperature between 300°F–350°F.

2 Place your pot on the grill directly over the coals.

3 To the pot, add all of the ingredients for the glaze.

4 Stir and simmer.

5 Remove from the grill and set aside.

6 Liberally coat the whole ham with your favorite pork seasoning.

7 Place the pineapple rings on the ham, holding them in place with the toothpicks.

8 Place a roasting pan with the rack inside on the side of the grill with no coals.

9 Put your ham into the pan.

10 Pour enough apple juice into the pan to cover the bottom.

11 Cover the grill with the lid. Total cook time will be about 5 hours, depending on the temperature of your grill.

12 After 1 hour, brush a layer of glaze onto the ham.

13 After 2½ hours, rotate the pan 180 degrees so the ham cooks evenly and apply another layer of glaze. Every 45 minutes to 1 hour after this, apply another layer of glaze.

14 When the internal temperature of the ham reaches 160°F, remove the ham from the grill.

15 Let the ham rest for 20 minutes to let the juices redistribute throughout the ham.

16 Slice the ham and put with your favorite fixin's.

17 Serve and enjoy!

SCAN &
WATCH

SCAN & WATCH

STUFFED PULLED PORK

Not all pulled pork is the same. Try this stuffed pork shoulder recipe that we turned into a pulled pork sandwich. Remember, this is all "low and slow," so kick back and put your feet up.

INGREDIENTS

FOR THE BURGER

- 8 lb pork shoulder (Boston butt)
- salami
- prosciutto
- capocollo
- hamburger buns
- coleslaw
- BBQ sauce

FOR THE RUB

- ¼ cup paprika
- 2 tbsp granulated onion
- ¼ cup raw sugar
- 1 tbsp cayenne pepper
- 2 tbsp SPG

FOR THE SPRAY

- 2 cups water
- 1 tbsp apple cider vinegar
- spray bottle

METHOD

1 Mix the dry rub ingredients well.

2 Trim off any excess fat and leave the fat cap in place on the pork butt.

3 Take a fillet knife and poke a few holes in the pork shoulder, make the incisions deep enough to plug each hole with a slice of cured meat.

4 Apply the dry rub all over the pork, cover it well as this is going to form the crust as it cooks.

5 Plan on it taking about 1 hour per pound of pork at around 250°F.

6 Pour about ⅔ chimney full of charcoal to your grill and light the remaining ⅓. Place the lit coals on TOP of the unlit coals. This will give you the slow burn you want to cook this pork butt.

7 Place a water pan on the fire level and fill it with water.

8 Place the pork butt on the grate OPPOSITE the hot coals for INDIRECT HEAT. Use a probe thermometer to monitor internal heat.

9 About every 45 minutes to an hour, spray the pork butt with the spray mix.

10 You can also add some wood chunks for some smoke. Don't use too much smoke, you only want to see a light clean smoke coming off the grill.

11 Be sure to rotate the pork every so often to help get an even cook.

12 Once the pork reaches an internal temperature of 190°F, the meat has become very tender. Take the pork off the grill and wrap it in heavy duty foil, then wrap it either in a blanket or place it in a cooler for about an hour, maybe an hour and a half. This will allow it cook to perfection. Then simply shred the meat, pulling it apart with two forks.

13 Once the pork is finished, unwrap it and place in a pan or large bowl. Use metal claws or forks to tear the meat into shreds, removing any bone.

14 Place a good scoop of pulled pork onto a hamburger bun and top with your favorite BBQ sauce, coleslaw, or any of your favorite toppings.

We're talking about some fine eatin'.

SCAN &
WATCH

APPLE BUTTER TENDERLOIN

INGREDIENTS

- 4 pork tenderloins, 1–1½ lb each

FOR THE STUFFING

- 1½ cups freshly made apple sauce
- 1 stick butter, softened
- 1 tbsp SPG seasoning
- 4 rashers bacon, pre-cooked
- 1 large onion, diced
- butcher's string

PITMASTER PRIVILEGE

We like to add another layer of flavor to the roast, so we paint the tenderloin all over with our favorite BBQ sauce!

Pork tenderloin is on the menu at the Pit. The BBQ Pit Boys use a two tied tenderloin roast technique that keeps the pork moist and tender. It's stuffed with our apple butter stuffing. And it's real easy to do with these simple tips. You have to check this recipe out.

METHOD

1 For all four tenderloins: trim back the tough silverskin layer of connective tissue using a sharp knife. Pull back the silverskin using a paper towel for better grip.

2 Pound out one side with a meat tenderizer then slice several times with a sharp knife - this helps the seasoning flavor travel into the meat.

3 Combine the butter and apple sauce, mix in a tablespoon of seasoning then work this into the cut side of the meat on each tenderloin.

4 Scatter diced onion over the apple butter mix on one of the tenderloins. Then place one of the other apple butter tenderloins on top, so the sauce sides are together.

5 Lay the bacon rashers on an apple butter tenderloin, and join with the last apple butter tenderloin (as above).

6 Place one tenderloin pair on six lengths of butcher's string, tie the strings around the tenderloin to keep the stuffing in. Trim excess string. Repeat for the second tenderloin pair; you now have two pairs of tenderloins.

7 Place both tenderloins on an oven tray and add some more SPG seasoning to both sides, place the tray onto the grill and cook opposite the hot coals at about 300°F—it's gonna take about 45–50 minutes. After about 20 minutes, rotate the tray for even cooking.

8 At this point you can also paint on some of your favorite BBQ sauce.

9 Cook to an internal temp of about 145°F, let them rest for a few minutes before serving.

10 Great served with mashed potatoes and string beans. You might want to make up some gravy from the drippings too.

SCAN & WATCH

LEG OF LAMB

Leg of lamb slow roasted with garlic and SPG and served with mashed potatoes and beer gravy makes for some fine eating at the Pit.

INGREDIENTS

FOR THE LAMB

- leg of lamb, bone in
- 8–10 garlic cloves, peeled
- 24 oz beer
- SPG seasoning, your favorite seasoning, or salt and pepper
- 2–3 onions, quartered

FOR THE MINT SAUCE

- 1 bunch fresh mint
- ½ tbsp of salt
- 8 tbsp of boiling water
- 4 tbsp white wine vinegar, or brown vinegar
- 1 tbsp of sugar

PITMASTER PRIVILEGE

We added some peach wood to the coals for some extra smoky flavor.

METHOD FOR LAMB

1 Leaving the fat on, make some holes in the meat with a sharp knife and plug them with whole garlic cloves.

2 Season well with SPG all over, place the lamb on the smoker, and cook at 275°F.

3 Place a drip pan underneath the leg of lamb to catch the drippings, add some beer to the drip tray to keep the moisture up, and throw in the onions and some garlic cloves. It's gonna be perfect to use for gravy.

4 After about 4 hours when the internal temp is around 120°F, take the leg of lamb off the grill, wrap it in some foil and then in a kitchen towel.

5 Let the lamb rest for about 45 minutes to continue cooking until it reaches about 130°F.

6 When cutting the lamb, any red liquid appearing is not blood, but myoglobin, the pigment that gives red meat it's color, so no need for concern.

7 Best served with mashed potatoes and gravy. You won't believe how good this lamb is with boiled, salted, and buttered peas, and a few sprigs of fresh mint. Eat and enjoy.

METHOD FOR MINT SAUCE

1 Strip the mint leaves off the stems, chop finely, and sprinkle with salt.

2 Place the chopped mint and salt into a bowl, add the sugar, and pour over the boiling water. Stir until dissolved and let it cool.

3 Stir in the vinegar once it's cooled down. You can add more water or vinegar if you want, just taste it first.

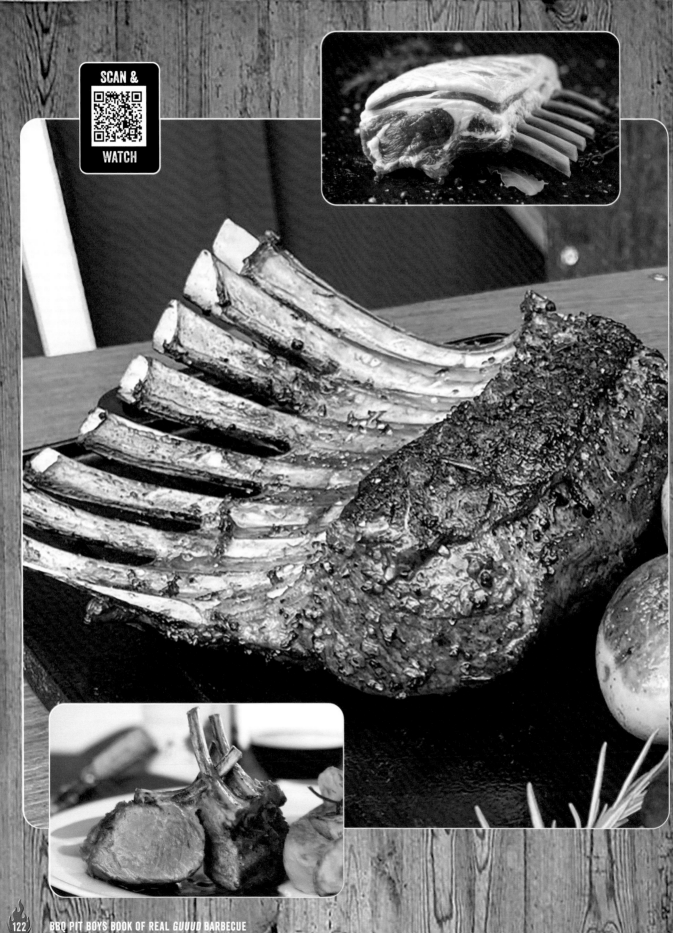

RACK OF LAMB

INGREDIENTS

- 1 French cut rack of lamb
- fresh mint, chopped
- fresh rosemary, chopped
- 4 tbsp butter
- SPG seasoning
- 10 cloves fresh garlic, smashed
- 1 lb par boiled potatoes
- approx. 3 cups fresh peas
- olive oil

Garlic goes real good with lamb!

This rack of lamb recipe is not just quick, but it's easy and real tasty too—with just a few ingredients and cooked over charcoal in just a few minutes.

METHOD

1 Take the rack of lamb and give it a good rub down with a quality oil like virgin olive oil.

2 Season with SPG seasoning or your favorite seasoning—at the very least, you should use salt, pepper, and garlic.

3 Chop the fresh rosemary finely and rub into the lamb.

4 Place the lamb over direct heat and sear all over for a couple of minutes.

5 Then move over indirect heat to cook. This isn't going to take long—about 8 minutes per side if your grill is set to around 375°F. Be sure to check the internal temperature as you go, and don't let it get much over 125°F before you take it off the grill.

6 Once you have it off the grill, cover for about ten minutes to let it rest and to let juices settle in. The temperature will continue to rise as it rests, so you will end up with a perfect medium rare. If you cut without the rest time you will lose moisture.

7 In a cast iron, pan add the parboiled potatoes, some rosemary, 3 tbsp of butter, and about ten cloves of fresh garlic. Place over direct heat to brown.

8 Chop the fresh mint, add to the peas with a tablespoon of butter, and heat.

9 Serve hot and enjoy!

SPIT ROAST LEG OF LAMB

INGREDIENTS

- 1 leg of lamb
- SPG seasoning (or salt, pepper, and garlic)
- mint sauce, see page 121
- mustard
- apple cider vinegar or beer

PITMASTER PRIVILEGE

We used SPG seasoning for this one, but you can go with any rub or seasoning mix you like.

Imagine sinking your teeth into a succulent leg of lamb, slow-roasted to perfection on a Spinfire rotisserie over smoky charcoal. The outer layer is crisp and with a light char, locking the rich and juicy flavors of the tender meat inside. With every bite, the savory aroma and melt-in-your-mouth texture transport you to a world of gastronomic bliss. This is not just any lamb roast, it's a masterpiece of backyard BBQ that will leave your taste buds dancing and your guests clamoring for more. Get ready for a feast that will tantalize your senses and leave you craving for seconds!

METHOD

1 Rub the leg of lamb with mustard to enable the seasoning to stick.

2 Apply a liberal coating of SPG seasoning all over the lamb, ensuring all the fat and meat is covered.

3 Preheat the grill to around 300°F and prepare the spit.

4 Place the leg of lamb on the skewer of the spit and secure it tightly.

5 Be sure the fire/coals are on one side of the spit roast only. This will enable a slow steady cook, with some relief for the meat on one side as it spins. If you place too many coals, the heat will be too intense and you won't be able to achieve the "low and slow" effect you're looking for to maximize moisture and prevent meat from drying out.

6 Place the spit on the grill and start the roast.

7 Spritz the meat every 30 minutes or so with apple cider vinegar, beer, or whatever you like.

8 Use a probe thermometer to monitor the temperature of the meat. When the internal temperature reaches 125°F, the lamb will be cooked to medium-rare. If you prefer a different level of doneness, adjust the internal finishing temperature accordingly.

9 Once the lamb is cooked, remove it from the spit, and let it rest for 10–15 minutes before carving.

10 Serve the spit roasted leg of lamb with mint sauce and enjoy!

Man, you gotta check these out!!

GRILLED LAMB CHOPS

INGREDIENTS

- 4 lamb loin chops, 1½ to 1¾ inch thick
- 6 small red potatoes, peeled
- 1 lb baby carrots
- 6 white boiler onions or 2 small onions, chopped
- 1 bunch asparagus—remove bottom quarter of stems
- 5–6 garlic cloves
- mint jelly
- fresh mint leaves
- water

FOR THE MARINADE

- ½ cup olive oil
- 1 tbsp prepared mustard
- 1 tbsp Worcestershire sauce
- 3 sprigs fresh thyme or ½ tsp dry thyme
- 2 tsp fresh ground pepper

Tender spring lamb loin chops served with fresh asparagus, potatoes, carrots, and onions hot off the grill make for a food feast fit for a holiday meal.

METHOD

1 Place the marinade ingredients in a bowl, mix well, and add the lamb loin chops. Coat the lamb with the marinade and let sit for 1 hour or longer.

2 Set up your grill for indirect grilling: hot coals on one side of the grill and no coals on the other side.

3 Place a cast iron pot filled halfway with water on the grill over the hot coals.

4 When the water boils, add the peeled potatoes to the pot. Cover the pot with the lid.

5 After 10 minutes, add the carrots and onions to the pot and continue simmering on the side of the grill with no coals.

6 Place the lamb chops on the grill directly over the hot coals.

7 Sear the lamb chops for 2 minutes per side, then move to the side of the grill with no coals to finish cooking. Cover the grill with the lid.

8 Place the asparagus on the grill directly over the hot coals and top with garlic cloves. Leave for 2 minutes, then move to the side of the grill with no coals.

9 Remove the pot of potatoes, carrots, & onions from the grill and set aside (the potatoes should be fork tender).

10 Check the internal temp of the lamb chops. You are looking for a temp of 135°F–140°F.

11 Cover the grill with the lid.

12 After 4 or 5 minutes, the asparagus is done.

13 Remove the lamb chops when they hit 135°F and let rest to redistribute the juices throughout the meat.

14 Place a lamb chop on a plate with potatoes, carrots, & onions. Top the chop with mint jelly and a fresh mint leaf.

15 Serve and enjoy!

SCAN &

WATCH

VENISON STEW

INGREDIENTS

- 2–4 lb venison (or rabbit, squirrel, beef, pork)
- 1–2 lb hot sausage
- 3 large onions, chopped
- 4 cloves garlic
- 2 large carrots, chopped
- 2 sticks celery, chopped
- 2 large potatoes, chopped
- 1 bell pepper, chopped
- 1 cup mushrooms, chopped
- flour for browning meat
- bacon
- SPG seasoning
- 8 cups beef stock
- beer

This open fire, slow simmered, game meat recipe is easy to make, and will surely become one of your favorite meat stews. This BBQ Pit Boys venison stew recipe is a favorite on the open fire. Substitute beef, pork, rabbit, squirrel for this classic, simple game recipe.

METHOD

1 Rub the venison with bacon fat, add spices, and then sear the meat over an open fire.

2 Next cut up the seared meat, coat with flour, and put the meat, garlic, 1 chopped onion, and bacon in a black iron pot over the hot coals.

3 When browned, add enough beef stock (and some beer) to cover the meat.

4 Cover the pot and then slow simmer the meat until tender. (Venison and other game meats may require several hours to tenderize.)

5 Add stock and beer as necessary.

6 Roughly chop the vegetables and sausages and add to the pot.

7 Cover with more beef stock and beer.

8 Simmer in a covered pot an additional hour or more, or until the vegetables are fork tender.

9 Serve with fresh bread.

Grab yourself a beer, kick back and relax...

BRAISED RABBIT WITH OLIVES

INGREDIENTS

- 3 lb rabbit, chopped
- 4–5 carrots, sliced
- 1 celery stalk, chopped
- 1 onion, chopped
- fresh leaf oregano, parsley, basil
- ½ cup of capers
- 1 cup Sicilean marinated pitted olives
- 1 cup green marinated pitted olives
- ¼ cup red wine
- ½ cup white vinegar
- pecorino romano grated cheese
- SPG seasoning
- ½ cup beer
- olive oil

An old-school version of coniglio stomparato (rabbit stampede), this is real easy to do with these few simple steps.

METHOD

1 Oil the baking pan, and single layer in the rabbit pieces.

2 Add the carrots, celery, onion, oregano, parsley, basil, and capers.

3 Now add the olives, wine, and vinegar.

4 Sprinkle with pecorino romano cheese and some SPG seasoning. Add the beer and drizzle with some olive oil.

5 Cover with foil and bake for about an hour with a grill temperature of about 300°F–325°F.

6 After an hour, rotate pan for even cooking. Leave foil off and cover grill. Leave for 1½–2 hours.

7 Stir ingredients in pan and bring meat to the top to help brown. Cover grill and leave for another hour or so.

8 Eat and enjoy with some fresh Italian or French bread.

We're eatin' good tonight, Martha..! Can you smell that..? It smells guuud..!

SCAN & WATCH

ALLIGATOR TENDERLOIN

INGREDIENTS

FOR THE JAMBALAYA

- 2 x 2½ lb alligator tenderloins
- 1 cup onions, chopped
- 1 cup green bell pepper, chopped
- 1 cup celery, chopped
- ½ head of garlic, crushed
- 2 tbsp olive oil
- 1 lb andouille sausage
- 1 stick of butter, chopped
- ½ cup of Crown Royal Black whiskey
- 1 lb of crawfish tails
- 1 tbsp of cayenne pepper
- 2 cups of white rice, boiled
- 1–2 tbsp maple syrup
- 2 lb approx. thin cut bacon

Stuffed with Andouille Sausage and Crawfish Jambalaya, A "behind the scenes" look at the BBQ Pit Boys Pit. Check out this Alligator recipe!

METHOD

1 Set up your grills for indirect cooking–hot coals on one side of the grill only, at a temperature of 250°F.

2 Chop the onion, celery, and pepper into small pieces. Crush the garlic.

3 Place the andouille sausage on the grill, away from the coals. Cook until it is nice and golden.

4 Flip the sausage and lay several strips of bacon on top of, and around it. Cover and continue to cook until done. Allow to cool a little then chop into small chunks.

5 In a large pan over the coals heat the olive oil. Add the chopped vegetables and sauté until soft but not browned.

6 Stir in the sausage chunks and then add the butter. Pour in the whiskey and cook until the butter has melted.

7 Stir in the crawfish tails. Cover and cook until the crawfish are thoroughly heated through.

8 Lay 5 or 6 slices of bacon side by side on a board, then "weave" 5 or 6 more slices in the opposite direction, alternately sitting behind and on top of the original bacon slices–to make a bacon "patch."

9 "Butterfly" the alligator tenderloin–gently slice the meat down its length, taking care not to cut all the way through. Repeat several times, either side of the first cut opening up the piece of meat more widely each time until it lies flat.

10 Spoon the stuffing into the tenderloin, lift up each side to close the meat over the stuffing. Lay the tenderloin on the bacon, roll so the bacon wraps it and secures the stuffing.

11 Cook on the grill away from the coals until it's golden and the internal temperature is 175°F. Halfway through cooking pour a little maple syrup over the top and continue to cook until it is done.

12 Serve hot, relax, and enjoy!

MUSHROOM RAGOUT WITH VENISON

INGREDIENTS

- 1 large onion, chopped
- 1 tomato, chopped
- 4 lb mixed mushrooms, any type, chopped
- 2 tbsp tomato paste
- 2 tsp dried oregano
- 1–2 tbsp SPG seasoning
- hot sauce (optional)
- 8 cloves garlic, sliced
- olive oil
- 1 cup red wine
- 2 lb venison backstrap
- 3 tbsp butter

Cold and hungry? A winter's day is perfect for a BBQ Pit Boys mushroom ragout loaded up with venison backstrap. Don't have any venison? This 'shroom recipe also works well with beef and pork, and it's real easy to do, too.

METHOD

1 Heat olive oil in a black iron pan and sauté the onions until translucent.

2 Add the mushrooms to the pan and season with SPG seasoning. Drizzle more olive oil on top and continue cooking to remove excess moisture.

3 Add 4 cloves of sliced garlic, the tomato paste, tomatoes, and oregano to the pan. Stir to combine.

4 Add red wine and stir, then simmer to reduce.

5 Cut the venison into medallions and butterfly each piece with a sharp knife.

6 Melt the butter in a cast iron pan over medium heat. Add the remaining garlic and the venison to cook slowly. Season with SPG seasoning. Flip the meat after a few minutes.

7 Transfer the venison to a cutting board to rest. Pour the butter, garlic, and drippings into the mushroom ragu pan.

8 After the venison has rested, cut it into bite-sized pieces and add to the mushroom ragu.

9 Return the pan to the stove, mix, and bring to a simmer.

10 Serve and enjoy!

All these flavors are going to come together real guuud!

SCAN & WATCH

BBQ PIT BOYS

SCAN & WATCH

STUFFED ALLIGATOR BBQ

INGREDIENTS

- 1 5-foot alligator, skinned and cleaned
- 1 bag cornbread stuffing
- 1 large sweet onion, diced
- 1 large green bell pepper, diced
- 3 stalks of celery, diced
- 4 carrots, diced
- 1 lb cleaned crawfish tails
- ½ lb andouille sausage, diced
- Cajun/Creole seasonings to taste
- Louisiana hot sauce—as much as you can stand!
- 2 oz bourbon
- 2 sticks butter
- 1 cup chicken broth
- 1 orange, sliced

Scan and watch the video for this one! The BBQ Pit Boys cook up a 5 foot gator, stuffed with crawfish and Andouille cornbread.

METHOD

1 Add the butter, onion, bell pepper, celery, carrots, hot sauce, and sausage to a large pot, mix well, and simmer over medium heat.

2 Once the vegetables and sausage cook down, add the crawfish tails, mix, and simmer.

3 Add bourbon, seasoning, chicken broth, and the cornbread stuffing.

4 Stuff the body cavity of your cleaned and skinned gator with the stuffing mix.

5 Stitch the gator closed with butcher's twine, then rub liberally with olive oil and your choice of Cajun seasoning.

6 Place on the grill at about 250°F. Total cooking time will be about 3–4 hours. For the first hour, tent with aluminum foil to retain moisture.

7 Remove the foil after the first hour. From this point on, baste or spritz every half hour to retain moisture.

8 Towards the end of the cook, top the alligator with orange slices.

9 Serve and enjoy!

Ain't nothin' better than hanging at the Pit with some good friends!

POULTRY

WHETHER IT'S CHICKEN, TURKEY, HEN, OR GOOSE—
WINGS, THIGHS OR BREASTS—WE KNOW THAT THE
BEST WAY TO COOK ANY BIRD IS BBQ PIT BOYS STYLE.
MAN, THERE'S SOME GUUUD EATING COMING YOUR WAY
RIGHT HERE. MAKE YOUR GRANDMA PROUD BY SERVING
UP BLACK IRON ROCK CORNISH GAME HENS, OR KICK IT
UP WITH OUR WINGS, NACHO STYLE: A TON OF FLAVOR,
AND THEY'RE REAL EASY TO DO!

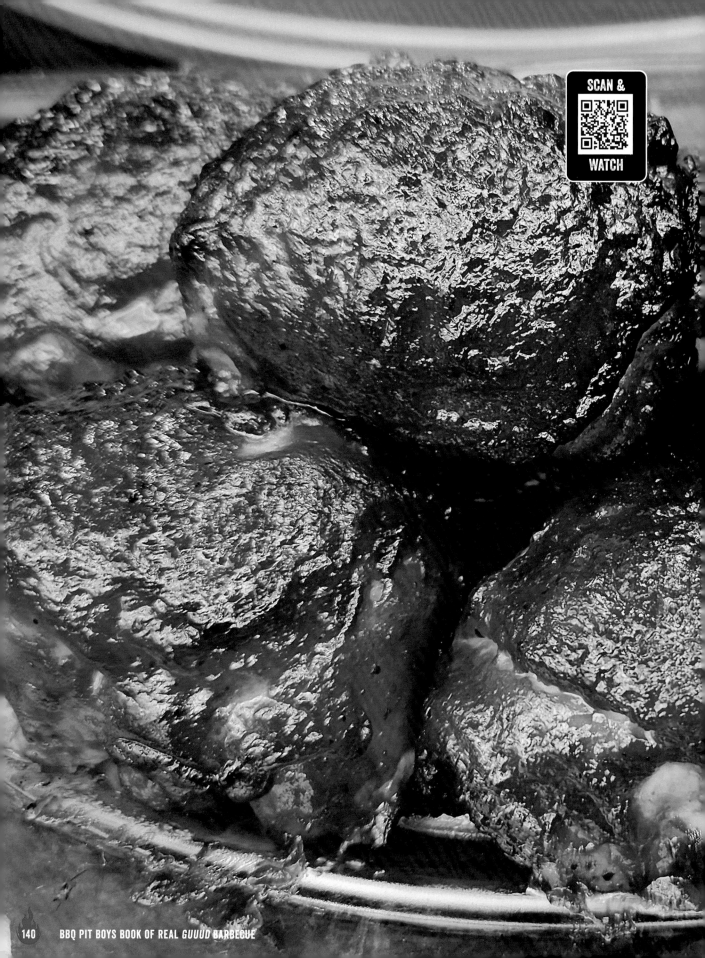

SCAN & WATCH

COMPETITION CHICKEN THIGHS

INGREDIENTS

- 8 chicken thighs, bone-in with skin on.
- poultry powder seasoning, or your favorite
- 1 stick butter
- ½ cup agave syrup
- ½ cup BBQ sauce

It's easy to make up some real tender and tasty chicken thighs on the barbecue grill, BBQ Pit Boys style.

METHOD

1 Loosen the skin, and cut off the knuckle to remove the bone from the thigh. You can also have your butcher prepare the thighs boneless, with skin on.

2 Trim some of the excess skin off the thigh. Season the meat on the underside of the thigh and roll up neatly.

3 Place a small pat of butter between the flesh and the skin. Wrap the skin around the thigh to hold the butter in place.

4 Place them in a mini loaf pan, similar to a muffin pan.

5 Combine the butter and agave syrup in a small pan and heat, stirring, until the butter melts.

6 Baste the thighs with the agave butter—or any sauce of your choice.

7 Grill indirectly at 275°F, basting regularly until done at an internal temperature of 165°F.

8 Submerge each thigh into your favorite BBQ sauce, then return to the grill to finish off and obtain the texture or char you want. Mop with the sauce as desired.

9 Serve as a snack or as a main meal.

Look at the glaze on that!

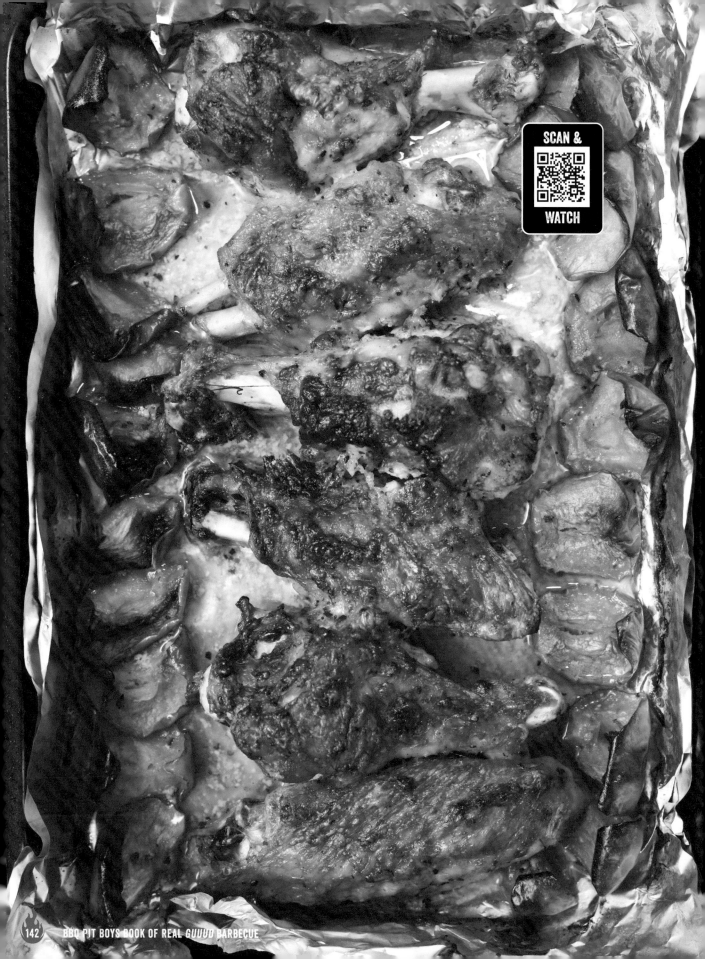

SMOKED TURKEY WINGS

INGREDIENTS

- 6 turkey wings
- olive oil
- hot BBQ sauce

FOR THE DRY RUB

- 1 tbsp cumin seed
- 1 tbsp fennel seed
- ½ tbsp sugar
- ½ tbsp salt
- 1 tbsp black pepper
- 1 tbsp cayenne
- 2 tbsp ground coriander
- 1 tbsp paprika
- 1 tbsp chili powder

These giant turkey wings are packed with meat and perfect for tailgating or simply at home on the grill.

METHOD

1 Combine all the dry rub ingredients in a bowl, mix well.

2 Cut off the wing tips if desired, place wings in a large bowl.

3 Pour some olive oil into the bowl and rub all over the wings.

4 Sprinkle on the dry rub mix, and rub evenly over the wings with your hands.

5 Place on a 325°F grill opposite the hot coals to cook.

6 When halfway through cooking, flip the wings to ensure even cooking. Add some wood chips to the fire for an added smokey flavor.

7 When just about cooked, brush some BBQ sauce on both sides of the wings, several times.

8 When wings reach an internal temp of 165°F, they are done.

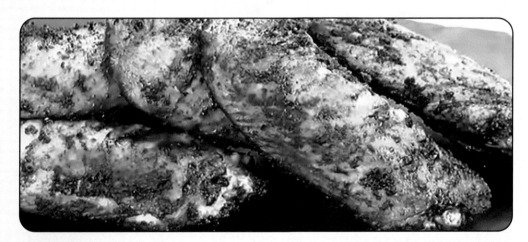

These ain't no puny chicken wings...

POUND CHICKEN

INGREDIENTS

- 2 x 4 lb whole chickens

FOR THE MARINADE

- ½ cup mayonnaise
- 1 tsp dried thyme
- 1 tsp garlic powder
- 1 tsp onion powder
- 1–2 tsp paprika
- 1 tsp kosher salt
- 1 tsp black pepper

FOR THE SECOND CHICKEN

- 1 bottle Italian dressing, your favorite brand

OR make our favorite recipe:

- 1–2 tsp oil
- 1 tsp vinegar
- 1 clove garlic, crushed
- 1 tsp salt
- 1 tsp ground black pepper
- 1 tsp dried thyme
- parmesan cheese, freshly grated
- ½ cup panko breadcrumbs

Black iron pans aren't just for cookin' in! So, grab yourself a couple of yard birds and your favorite iron pan, gonna be some good eatin' at the Pit tonight!

METHOD

1 Prepare the chickens: "butterfly" them by removing the back bone using a pair of boning shears or scissors. Hold the tail end and cut along both sides of the spine, then remove it. Trim back the protruding rib ends. Be careful as the shears will also cut fingers!

2 Combine marinade ingredients in a bowl, mix well.

3 With your fingers, cover one chicken with the marinade—spread liberally under the skin of the body and the legs.

4 For the second chicken, pour some Italian dressing under the skin and rub it in all over.

5 Bring grill temperature up to 375°F with coal offset for indirect cooking.

6 Place each chicken on a hard surface, cover with plastic wrap, and pound each chicken directly in the center of the breast bone 5–6 times with a cast iron skillet. This compresses the breast, ensuring the chickens cook evenly.

7 Allow the chickens to marinate in the seasoning—place in a bowl in the refrigerator. After 2 hours, cook them on the grill opposite the hot coals. Make sure the upper (skin) side is up and legs are facing toward the coals.

8 Rub in more Italian dressing over the second chicken and grate fresh parmesan cheese on top, then sprinkle panko breadcrumbs on top for a crispy texture.

9 Cover the grill and cook for 30 minutes, then rotate each chicken for even cooking. Cover the grill again, cook for another 30 minutes until internal temperature reaches 175°F.

10 Cut each chicken in half. Sear the chicken pieces directly over hot coals for 1–2 minutes. Do not overcook the chicken.

11 Place on plates and serve with sweet juicy corn!

SCAN &
WATCH

Man, these are going to be HOT!

SCAN & WATCH

Rated R for Vegematics!

GRILLED CHIPOTLE CHICKEN

INGREDIENTS

FOR THE MARINADE

- 2 lb boneless chicken breast, pounded (as needed)
- 2 x 7 oz cans chipotle peppers in adobo sauce
- ½ tsp cumin
- 2 tbsp paprika
- 1 tbsp chili powder
- salt, to taste
- 1 onion, chopped
- 4 garlic cloves, crushed
- ⅓ cup olive oil (or of your choice)
- 2 Italian bread loaves, halved (as needed)
- 4 tbsp mayonnaise (as needed)

Heat it up at the Pit with this tender and moist chipotle chicken stuffed sandwich.

METHOD

1 In a large mixing bowl, combine the chicken, the chipotle peppers, and all the spices: cumin, paprika, chili powder, salt, onion, and garlic. Add the olive oil and stir well to combine. Set aside for 2 hours to marinate.

2 Meanwhile, preheat the grill to a medium temperature.

3 When ready, place the chicken pieces on the grill and cook over direct flame until done, flipping regularly.

4 Scoop out the middle of the bread loaf to create a cavity. Spoon half of the mayonnaise into the cavity of one of the half loaves and then stuff it with chicken.

5 Serve and enjoy!

CHICKEN WING LOAF

INGREDIENTS

- 10 lb chicken wings (about 30)
- ½ cup vegetable oil (as needed)
- ¼ cup soy sauce (as needed)
- 2 tbsp favorite seasoning, to taste
- 1 cup BBQ sauce, or a sauce of your preference (as needed)
- 2 tbsp jalapeño pepper, chopped (or any preferred topping)
- ½ cup mozzarella, shredded and cheddar (as needed)

PITMASTER PRIVILEGE

You can use any sauce you like for cookin' up this chicken.

Tired of regular style chicken wings? We stack the wings (lefty and righty) to keep them moist and tender.

METHOD

1 Preheat grill to 275°F.

2 In a bowl, combine vegetable oil, soy sauce, and seasoning. Mix well and baste the chicken with the mixture.

3 Stack chicken on the grill over indirect heat. Cover and cook for about 2 hours.

4 After an hour, baste the chicken wings with BBQ sauce (or the sauce of your choice). Continue to cook.

5 In the last few minutes of cooking, sprinkle the jalapeño peppers (or your preferred topping) and the cheese on top.

6 Cover and cook until the cheese melts.

7 Serve hot and enjoy!

Can you smell that?

SCAN & WATCH

...it smells guuud!

SCAN & WATCH

NACHO WINGS

INGREDIENTS

- 6 lb whole chicken wings
- hot sauce, your favorite
- 1–2 tbsp taco seasoning, your favorite
- 4 green onions, chopped
- 1 bunch cilantro, chopped
- 1 large tomato, diced
- 1 bag nacho chips, your favorite
- 2 lb cheese—cheddar plus one other, shredded
- 1 small can of black beans
- black olives, sliced (as needed)
- 1 onion, finely chopped
- 1 small jar jalapeño peppers, sliced
- 1 lime, to serve
- pico de gallo salsa, to serve
- guacamole, to serve
- sour cream, to serve

PITMASTER PRIVILEGE

You're gonna need some cerveza for the Pitmaster!

Hold off on those same ol' same ol' boring Buffalo wings for your next tailgate or pit party...enough is enough, so kick it up this time and try these wings, nacho style. A ton of flavor, and they're real easy to do!

METHOD

1 Place the chicken wings in large bowl. (Keep the wing tips, it gives you something to hold when eating!)

2 Pour some hot sauce all over the wings.

3 Add the taco seasoning. Mix well together with your hands, coating all wings with the seasoning.

4 Turn out onto a sheet pan, spread evenly, and arrange the wings so the top side faces up.

5 Place the wings on grill to cook away from the coals. Halfway through the cooking time, about 20 minutes, rotate the pan for even cooking.

6 While the wings are cooking, chop your the green onions and cilantro, and very finely chop the tomato.

7 Place the nacho chips in plastic bag and smash them into tiny bits with your fist.

8 When the wings are cooked, sprinkle the cheese all over them followed by the crushed nacho chips. Replace the grill cover and cook until the cheese has melted and the topping is golden and crunchy.

9 Sprinkle the olives, jalapeños, black beans, green onions, cilantro, onion, and tomato evenly over the chicken dish.

10 Squeeze the lime juice over everything.

11 Serve with guacamole, sour cream, and salsa. Enjoy!

SCAN & WATCH

BUFFALO WINGS GRILLED CHICKEN STYLE

INGREDIENTS

- 6 lb whole chicken wings
- hot sauce, homemade or store bought, as needed
- olive or vegetable oil
- SPG seasoning, or your favorite seasoning mix

PITMASTER PRIVILEGE

You can add some of your favorite hot pepper sauce to the hot sauce if it isn't hot enough for your taste!

The BBQ Pit Boys show you how easy it is to grill up some smoking hot or mild smoked Buffalo wings!

METHOD

1 Put a pan of homemade or your favorite store bought hot sauce to warm on the grill.

2 Wash and dry the wings. Do not cut off the wing tips.

3 Coat the wings in oil and SPG seasoning, or your favorite chicken rub.

4 Sear the wings for a couple of minutes on each side over the hot coals.

5 Move the wings to the other side of the grill for indirect heating, opposite the coals. Add some hardwood such as hickory to the coals for an additional smoky flavor.

6 Cover in a 350°F grill for about 30 minutes. Halfway through, flip the wings to ensure even cooking.

7 Remove the wings when when the internal temperature reaches 165°F. Cooking time will vary depending on the size of the wings and how hot your grill is.

8 Serve with your favorite hot or mild barbeque sauce.

They're mighty fine eatin'!

CHICKEN DRAGON EGGS

INGREDIENTS

- 1 skinless boneless chicken breast
- 5–6 slices pork belly bacon
- 1 tbsp cream cheese
- 1 green jalapeño pepper
- 2 oz (approx.) shredded cheddar cheese
- favorite seasoning for a rub
- favorite sauce for basting

No eggs required for these bacon wrapped jalapeno popper stuffed chicken breasts. Pitmaster of the Joseph-Que chapter put this together using these simple tips.

METHOD

1 Cut the jalapeño in half lengthwise and remove the seeds and inner stem.

2 "Butterfly" the chicken breast by slicing horizontally through the depth of the breast. Open it up to flatten it out.

3 Place a plastic wrap over the opened up chicken breast and bash it out with the smooth side of a meat mallet. This makes the meat an even thickness and tenderizes it.

4 Fill both the hollowed out jalapeño halves with cream cheese, add a good layer of shredded cheese on top, and join the halves together. You now have a perfect "dragon egg."

5 Place the dragon egg in the middle of the flattened chicken and wrap the chicken around the pepper.

6 Take a strip of pork belly bacon and start wrapping it tightly around the chicken dragon egg. Continue until the entire chicken breast has been wrapped with the bacon strips. Trim the edges to tidy up if you want.

7 Take your favorite seasoning and rub it all over the bacon-wrapped chicken.

8 Place the bacon-wrapped chicken over indirect heat, and cook until the internal temperature to be about 165°F.

9 You may baste the breast in some sauce during cooking, and do it several times as you want.

10 Take the "dragon egg" off the grill and let it set for a few minutes. Enjoy!

Are you getting hungry or what?

CHICKEN PIG CHEESE WRAPS

INGREDIENTS

- 6 chicken breasts
- BBQ Pit Boys Poultry Powder
- 3 tbsp (approximately) dijon mustard
- 6 slices swiss cheese
- 12 breakfast sausages, pre-cooked
- flour, for coating
- 3–4 eggs, whisked
- panko breadcrumbs
- cooking oil

No more tasteless and dry boneless chicken breasts. Wrap some pounded out boneless chicken breasts around some pork sausage and cheese and then grill. It's easy to do with these simple tips.

METHOD

1 Bring grill temperature up to 300°F, with coals offset for indirect cooking.

2 Trim up and butterfly the chicken breasts. With one palm on the breast, using a sharp knife, slice horizontally through the depth of the breast and open it up to flatten it out.

3 Using the smooth side of a meat mallet, lightly pound the chicken breasts to tenderize and flatten them evenly.

4 Coat the chicken in poultry powder rub. Spread some mustard on the chicken. We use a mixture of mustard and horseradish.

5 Add a slice of swiss cheese and place two breakfast sausages, end to end, on top of the cheese.

6 Roll up the chicken breast and tie tight with some twine.

7 Put the flour in a wide, shallow dish and season well with the poultry powder, or your favorite seasoning.

8 Roll the chicken breasts in the flour, then in the egg wash, and finally through the breadcrumbs.

9 In a pan on the grill, heat up some cooking oil and fry the chicken on both sides to get a nice crust.

10 Place the seared chicken wraps in a pan and cook in your smoker or oven at 325°F until an internal temperature of 165°F is reached, about 40 minutes.

11 Top with your favorite sauce for a little extra flavor and moisture. Enjoy!

It's real easy to do!

HOT WING KEBABS

INGREDIENTS

- 6 lb chicken wings, cut into wingettes and drummettes
- green onions, chopped, for serving

FOR THE BASTE

- 6 tbsp ketchup
- 3 tbsp soy sauce
- 1 tbsp habanero chipotle sauce (or your favorite hot sauce)
- 4 tbsp brown sugar
- 3 tbsp white vinegar

PITMASTER PRIVILEGE

We went with habanero chipotle, but you can use any hot sauce you like for grillin' up this chicken.

Hot wing kebabs / kabobs / kebobs—call 'em what you like, these quick and easy chicken wings are real tasty and perfect for snacking and as a side, or make a bunch of them as part of a main course.

METHOD

1 Use flat skewers; these are better than the round form because the meat doesn't spin on the skewer.

2 Thread the wingettes onto skewers. Then thread the drumettes onto skewers. It's best to keep them separate as they need slightly different cooking times. Also be sure to leave a small space between each piece of meat to allow for even cooking.

3 Combine all the baste ingredients in a bowl and baste the chicken pieces.

4 Cook over direct heat. Rotate and baste often, for even cooking. Ensure you have a good gap between the heat source and the chicken. Use metal skewers if you can, they don't burn out or catch fire like the bamboo skewers.

5 Cook until browned and an internal temperature of 165°F is reached.

6 Serve hot with freshly chopped green onion sprinkled on top.

Oh, Man! Take a look at that!

SCAN &
WATCH

BBQ PIT BOYS

BBQ PIT BOYS

CHICKEN CHEESE THIGHS

INGREDIENTS

- 8 bone-in, skin-on chicken thighs
- Sweet Martha rub (or your favorite seasoning)
- vegetable or olive oil
- cheese, shredded
- SPG seasoning
- Smoky Whiskey BBQ sauce, or your favorite, to serve

FOR THE MOP

- 6 oz beer
- 3–4 tbsp Sweet Martha rub or your favorite seasoning

Chicken thighs deserve more respect, and these cheesy chicken morsels will do it just fine. Try this recipe and see how quick and easy it is to do.

METHOD

1 Preheat your grill to about 325°F–350°F.

2 Coat the thighs with the vegetable oil. Massage some Sweet Martha rubx (or your preferred seasoning) over all sides of the meat.

3 Place the thighs skin side up, opposite the coals for indirect cooking. Cover and cook.

4 Make the mop by combining the beer and some Sweet Martha seasoning in a bowl.

5 After about 15 minutes, baste the thighs with the Sweet Martha mop.

6 Wait about another 10 minutes, flip the thighs to skin-side down, and sprinkle some SPG seasoning over the top. Cook for another 10 minutes.

7 Mop the thighs one more time and move them to sit directly over the coals, skin side down, to sear the skin.

8 When seared, after a couple of minutes, move them off the direct heat. Turn them over so they are skin side up and place a handful of shredded cheese on top of each of them.

9 Cover the grill to melt the cheese.

10 When internal temperature reaches 165°F, remove from the grill and serve with the barbecue sauce of your choice and your favorite sides. Enjoy!

You gotta check this out!

SCAN &
WATCH

BBQ PIT BOYS
...And - in the
Miracle of time...

APPLE CIDER SMOKED TURKEY

INGREDIENTS

- 1 x 14 lb turkey
- poultry seasoning
- ¼ cup extra virgin olive oil (as needed)
- 1 bottle ale
- ¼ cup melted butter (as needed)
- big bag of ice cubes

FOR THE BRINE

- 16 cups apple cider/apple juice
- 1 cup kosher salt
- 1 cup dark brown sugar
- 8–10 garlic cloves, smashed
- ½ cup sliced ginger
- 4 oranges, quartered
- ⅓ cup apple cider vinegar
- 8 cups water (as needed)
- 2 tbsp chili pepper flakes
- 2 sprigs fresh rosemary
- 2 sprigs fresh thyme
- 2 sprigs fresh sage

Crispy, moist, and tender turkey from the grill is easy to do—especially with this apple cider and brown sugar brine recipe.

METHOD

1 In a saucepan, combine apple cider/juice, salt, and brown sugar. Heat until sugar dissolves.

2 Into a large clean bucket, pour the cider mixture, followed by just enough water to cover the turkey.

3 Add apple cider vinegar, garlic, ginger, orange, and chili pepper flakes.

4 Put fresh rosemary, thyme, and sage into the turkey cavity.

5 Lower the turkey into the bucket with brine. Add a bag of ice, cover, and set the bucket aside for 18–24 hours.

6 The following day, preheat grill to 300°F–325°F.

7 Remove the turkey from brine and place on a roasting pan. Remove the herbs from cavity and pat dry with paper towel.

8 Baste turkey with olive oil, season lightly with poultry seasoning or your favorite seasoning.

9 Pour ale in the roasting pan and place the turkey in the pan, breast side down.

10 Place the roasting pan on the grill, cover, and cook for 80 minutes.

11 Turn the turkey over, baste with pan juices, and cook breast side up for another 2½ hours.

12 Baste again with pan juice and continue to cook for another hour.

13 Brush some melted butter over the turkey to make the skin crispy and cook until the internal temperature reaches 160°F, basting once or twice with pan juice in between.

14 Remove the turkey from heat and place on a cutting board. Tent the meat with foil and let rest for about an hour.

15 Carve, serve, and enjoy!

WILD GOOSE BREAST

INGREDIENTS

- 2 goose breasts, fresh
- 6 cups water
- 1 cup salt, non-iodized

FOR THE CHAIRMAN GOOSE MARINADE

- 2 tbsp ponzu sauce
- 4 tbsp sweet & sour sauce
- 1½ tbsp pickled ginger
- 2½ tbsp sriracha sauce
- 2 tbsp toasted sesame seeds
- 4 tbsp Worcestershire sauce
- 1½ tbsp Emeril's Asian Essence
- resealable plastic bag

Call in the geese. An environmental problem solved when you cook up some wild Canadian goose breast on the grill. Over 90% of the meat in a goose is the breast, so many hunters use the "breast-out" method when preparing geese for a meal.

METHOD

1 Remove feathers from the sternum breast area by pulling them off until the sternum is exposed.

2 Run a sharp knife along sternum to expose the breast meat and cut the breast meat out of each goose.

3 Combine water and salt in a large storage container to make the brine. Place the goose breasts in the brine for 24–30 hours.

4 After 24–30 hours, remove the breasts from the brine and lay each breast flat on a cutting board. Slice each breast in half horizontally to make two thin breasts, four pieces in all.

5 Take a meat tenderizer and pound each breast to make thin and to tenderize.

6 "Fork" each breast by stabbing each breast all over with a fork, to help tenderize. You can also use a commercial "blade" meat tenderizer.

7 Combine the marinade ingredients in a resealable plastic bag.

8 Place each tenderized breast in the marinade and turn them over in the bag to mix thoroughly. Leave to marinate 12–24 hours in the refrigerator or cooler.

9 Bring the grill temperature up to 350°F–400°F, with coals to the side for indirect cooking.

10 Once marinated, place the goose breasts on the grill opposite the hot coals, cover, and cook for 20 minutes.

11 Flip the breasts over, cover, and cook for a further 10 minutes maximum. Remove and place on a plate.

12 Serve with fresh corn on the cob, a salad of tomato, cucumber, and onion, and roasted potatoes.

13 Sit back, relax, and enjoy!

There's some real guuud eating right there...

POULTRY ★ WILD GOOSE BREAST

CORNISH GAME HENS

INGREDIENTS

- 3 x 2 lb Cornish game hens, with giblets
- 2 sprigs rosemary
- 1 onion, chopped
- cooking oil
- 2 celery stalks, cut into sticks
- 2 carrots, cut into sticks
- 12 small red potatoes, cut in half for faster cooking
- 8–10 cloves garlic, peeled
- ½–1 cup baby corn, optional
- 6 tbsp butter
- chicken stock
- salt and pepper, to taste
- 2 tbsp lemon juice
- ½ cup white wine
- 2 tbsp butter for the gravy
- 3–4 tsp corn starch

Make your grandma proud by serving up these Black Iron Rock Cornish Game Hens at your next Barbecue.

METHOD

1 Set up your grill for indirect grilling with hot coals on one side of the grill and no coals on the other side. You are aiming for a temperature of 350°F.

2 Place the skillet on the side of the grill with no coals.

3 Remove the giblets from the hens and put the rosemary sprigs and some chopped onion into the body cavity.

4 Place the hens into the skillet breast side up, rub cooking oil all over, and surround with all of the vegetables, including the garlic and the baby corn, if using.

5 Place cubes of butter on top and pour over just enough broth to cover the bottom of the skillet. Season with salt and pepper. Cover the grill to cook.

6 After a few minutes, add the lemon juice and wine to the skillet. Re-cover grill and continue cooking.

7 Every 15 or 20 minutes, baste the hens with the juices in the pan and rotate the skillet 180 degrees for even cooking.

8 Hens will be done when temperature at the thigh registers 180°F, after about 1 hour.

9 Take 1 cup of juice from the pan and put into a cooking pot to start making the gravy. Place the pot of pan juices on the grill and re-cover the grill.

10 Chop up the giblets, add them to the pot, and simmer.

11 Add butter to the gravy, let it melt, then add 3 tsp of corn starch to the gravy and stir well to thicken.

12 Remove the hens from the grill and place on a serving platter. Surround the birds with the vegetables and pour the gravy over the birds and veggies.

13 Serve and enjoy!

SCAN &
WATCH

GRILLED PHEASANT

INGREDIENTS

- 2–4 wild pheasants, ask your butcher to prepare if you prefer not to do it yourself
- 1½ cups maple syrup
- SPG seasoning, to taste
- 1–2 cups apple sauce

PITMASTER PRIVILEGE

You can use any rub you like for grillin' up this pheasant. If you want the same tastes as this recipe and don't have SPG, use garlic, salt, and pepper.

Fresh grilled pheasant is on the menu at the Pit. A fall season favorite, apple maple pheasant. And it's real easy to do!

METHOD

1 Bring grill temperature up to 275°F–300°F.

2 Pluck and clean the pheasants and separate leg quarters and breasts, unless your butcher supplies them already prepared.

3 Rinse well with water.

4 Apply maple syrup to each leg quarter and each breast.

5 Coat all with a generous amount of SPG seasoning.

6 Place leg quarters and breasts directly over hot coals, cover grill, and cook. Flip the pheasant pieces often.

7 When leg quarters and breasts reach an internal temperature of 155°F–160°F, turn one more time and apply a coating of apple sauce.

8 Cover the grill and cook long enough for the apple sauce to heat up.

9 Remove the pheasant pieces from the grill to a cutting board. Leave to rest for 5–8 minutes.

10 Serve with mashed potatoes, green beans, or stuffing.

11 Sit back, relax, and enjoy!

Remove everything that doesn't look like meat!

SCAN & WATCH

It's about time to eat!

COCONUT CHICKEN DRUMSTICKS

INGREDIENTS

- 15 chicken drumsticks
- 1 tbsp brown sugar
- sea salt
- 2 tsp smoked paprika
- 1 tbsp onion powder
- 2 green coconuts, for fresh coconut juice (otherwise canned will do)
- 1 lime, zested
- 2–4 fresh red chili peppers, chopped
- 2 tbsp fresh root ginger, chopped

FOR THE BASTING SAUCE

- 1 tbsp sea salt
- 2–4 fresh red chili peppers, chopped
- fresh cilantro, chopped
- 2 tsp smoked paprika
- 2 anchovies
- juice of 1 lime
- 4 tbsp coconut oil

Fresh green coconut juice and lime zest make these grilled chicken drumsticks as juicy as ever with just a few simple steps, —you're gonna love these!

METHOD

1 Put the drumsticks into a large baking pan.

2 Add the brown sugar, salt, paprika, and onion powder.

3 Pour the coconut juice over the drumsticks. Add lime zest, chili pepper, and ginger. Set aside for at least an hour in the refrigerator.

4 In a bowl, combine all of the basting ingredients and mash them up together—use a pestle and mortar if you have one.

5 Arrange drumsticks neatly on the grill over indirect heat.

6 Cook, basting regularly (every 10–15 minutes) with the sauce. When an internal temp of 165°F is reached, the drumsticks are done.

7 Remove the drumsticks from the grill to a serving dish or tray. Squeeze a little more lime juice over the tray, and add some cilantro.

8 Serve and enjoy!

BBQ PIT BOYS

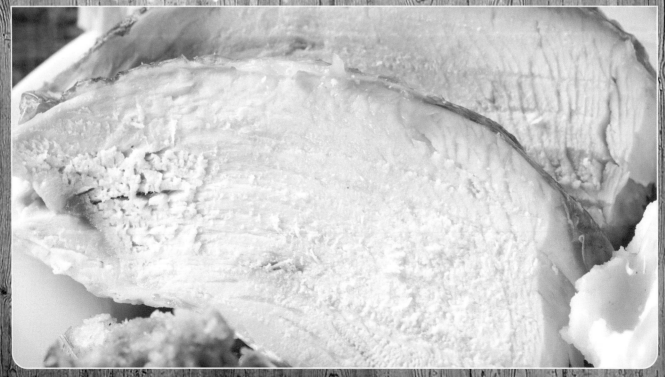

SMOKED BONELESS TURKEY BREAST

INGREDIENTS

- **10 lb boneless turkey breast (no more than 10% brining solution added)**
- **chicken broth**
- **SPG seasoning, to taste**

FOR INJECTION MARINADE:

- **1 stick butter, unsalted**
- **½ tsp garlic powder**
- **¼ cup chicken broth**
- **½ tsp Bell's seasoning**

This easy-to-smoke boneless turkey breast has just a few simple ingredients and tastes great.

METHOD

1 Bring the smoker temperature up to 300°F. Use your favorite smoking wood or pellets.

2 Place a pan over hot coals and add the ingredients for the injection marinade. Stir constantly as it heats up.

3 Fill meat injector with marinade and inject breast in 10–15 different places.

4 Apply SPG liberally to the breast.

5 Place the turkey breast in a roasting pan on the smoker.

6 Add ½ cup of chicken broth to the bottom of the pan. Insert an external thermometer into the top of the breast.

7 Periodically check to make sure there is broth in the bottom of the pan, and add broth as needed.

8 Remove the breast from the smoker when an internal temperature of 160°F is reached.

9 Place the breast on a cutting board and cover with aluminum foil, let it rest 15–20 minutes. Then uncover and remove any strings holding the breast together.

10 Carve the breast and serve with stuffing, mashed potatoes, gravy, rolls, corn, green bean casserole, and cranberry sauce.

11 Sit back, relax, and enjoy!

This is some guuud eatin'!

SCAN & WATCH

THAI STICK CHICKEN WINGS

INGREDIENTS

- 6 lb chicken wings, separated into drumettes and wingettes (for even cooking)
- 2½ cups coconut milk
- 1 tbsp peanut butter
- ⅔ cup crushed peanuts
- 1 tbsp cayenne pepper
- 2 fresh red chili peppers,
- 2 fresh green chili peppers,
- 1 bunch fresh cilantro
- 1 fresh lime
- skewers

Raise your swords and check out these BBQ Pit Boys chicken wings grilled on skewers. This chicken recipe is real easy to do for tailgating and at your pit.

METHOD

1 Combine the coconut milk, peanut butter, one of the green peppers, and cayenne pepper powder in a blender or food processor and blend well.

2 Thread the chicken wingettes onto one skewer, keeping a little space between each wingette for even cooking. Repeat exactly the same method for the drumettes.

3 Baste the skewered chicken with the basting sauce and place over a charcoal fire, far enough away to allow time to cook reasonably slowly.

4 Baste and rotate the chicken regularly. The constant rotation and basting ensures the meat is moist and tender.

5 Finely chop the green and red chilies and the cilantro.

6 Once cooked, take the chicken skewers off the grill to a chopping board.

7 Finely grate lime zest over the wings, add a good coating of finely chopped cilantro, the chopped red and green chili peppers, and the crushed peanuts.

8 Serve hot with plenty of cold beer.

It don't get any better than this, right?

TURKEY WITH STUFFING AND WILD TURKEY GRAVY

INGREDIENTS

- 13 x lb fresh turkey (small enough to fit in your grill)
- 1 lemon, halved
- 1 tangerine, quartered
- olive oil
- marjoram, to taste
- thyme, to taste
- rosemary, to taste
- chicken broth
- butcher's string

FOR THE STUFFING & GRAVY

- 1 stick of butter
- 1 onion, chopped
- 4 oz mushrooms, sliced
- 1 celery stick. sliced
- turkey giblets, finely chopped
- 2 cups chicken stock
- 1 packet bread stuffing mix
- salt and pepper, to taste
- 1 tbsp corn starch
- 1 oz Wild Turkey whiskey (or your favorite)
- water

Save the kitchen oven for the pies and cook your turkey, giblet stuffing, and Wild Turkey gravy on the old charcoal grill. It not only is moist, tender, and delicious, but it's easy to do with these tips!

METHOD

1 Lightly brown the onions, celery, and mushrooms in butter in a black iron pan over the hot coals. Add the chopped giblets to the pan and cook for a few minutes more.

2 Add the chicken stock to the pan followed by your favorite bread stuffing mix, heat thoroughly. Make the stuffing very moist—add more stock as necessary, then remove from heat.

3 Prepare the turkey: squeeze the lemon and rub the juice all over the turkey (this is thought to open up the pores). Throw some salt into the cavity of the bird and then stuff with the hot stuffing.

4 Place a baking pan with a rack inside on the grill, away from the coals. Pour some stock into the bottom of the pan.

5 Tie the legs together with some string, and tie the wings against the body of the bird, to help keep them moist.

6 Place the turkey breast side down on the rack in the pan. Drizzle and rub on some oil and then the herbs and seasoning.

7 Add a little hardwood to the coals for a smoky flavor. Roast indirectly in a 275°F–325°F closed grill for about 4 hours.

8 Halfway through, rotate the pan to ensure even cooking. Baste the turkey every half hour or so. Flip the turkey to brown the breast side. Place the tangerine on the coals.

9 Cook until the meat reaches 180°F at its thickest part near the leg bone. The stuffing should be at least 145°F. Remove from the pan and leave to rest for about 20 minutes.

10 Make a paste with the corn starch and water, stir into the roasting pan, and add some wild turkey to make the gravy.

11 Serve with your favorite side dishes, relax, and enjoy!

SCAN & WATCH

Super easy, super tasty!

This is about
as good as it
gets!

CHILI CHICKEN SUB

INGREDIENTS

- 3 boneless chicken breasts
- 1 tomato, sliced
- 1 bread loaf or baguette
- BBQ sauce

FOR THE MARINADE

- 2 garlic cloves, finely chopped
- 3 Anaheim chili peppers
- 2 red chili peppers, deseeded and chopped finely
- 1 tbsp paprika
- 1 tbsp salt
- ½ tbsp black pepper
- ½ tbsp white pepper
- 1 tbsp sesame oil
- 2 eggs

Chicken and chili go together, no doubt about it. If you're looking for a great chicken sandwich to grill up at your pit, check this easy to do recipe out.

METHOD

1 Put the sesame oil in a large bowl, add the garlic, paprika, salt, white, and black pepper.

2 Break the egg whites into the bowl—you can reserve the yolk for another dish. Add de-seeded and chopped red chili peppers. Mix well.

3 Slice the chicken breasts horizontally depthwise, so they are the same size but thinner pieces. Try to use small chicken breasts, they're more tender.

4 Add the sliced chicken breasts to the marinade, stir to cover the chicken thoroughly, set aside for about 20 minutes.

5 Roast the Anaheim peppers over direct heat until charred, set aside to cool.

6 Add some oil to the grill and cook the chicken pieces on the grill or hibachi over a high heat until they reach an internal temperature of 165°F. A few minutes per side.

7 Cut the Anaheim chili peppers in half lengthwise and deseed. Remove some of the charred skin if wanted.

8 Take the chicken off the grill and dust with paprika.

9 Place in a good sub bread roll or french baguette with sliced tomatoes, roasted Anaheim peppers, and BBQ sauce.

10 Relax and enjoy!

SALMON WITH GINGER CHILI SAUCE

INGREDIENTS

FOR THE SALMON

- 2 x 1½ lb salmon fillets
- 2–3 tsp olive oil

FOR THE SAUCE

- ½ cup water
- ½ cup rice vinegar
- 1 tbsp soy sauce
- 1 tbsp chili paste/sauce
- 4 cloves garlic, minced
- 2 tbsp ginger, minced
- 4 tbsp brown sugar
- 2 tbsp butter

Grilled salmon fillet basted with a ginger and chili sauce makes for some good eating at the Pit. And it's real quick and easy to do!

METHOD

1 Bring grill temperature up to 350°F with coals offset for indirect cooking.

2 Combine all ingredients for ginger chili sauce in a sauce pan and place directly over hot coals.

3 Heat until it reaches a simmer, stirring often.

4 Coat the salmon fillet with olive oil on the skin side only, and place on a cookie sheet skin side down.

5 Spoon 3–4 tablespoons of ginger chili sauce over fillets.

6 Place pan opposite hot coals for indirect cooking.

7 Cover and cook. Every 10 minutes, remove cover and baste with more ginger chili sauce.

8 Cover and let cook another 10–15 minutes.

9 Remove lid and check for doneness. Fish should be soft and flakey. If they are firm, cover and cook another 5–10 minutes.

10 Use a spatula to cut fish into portions while still on the pan.

11 Remove and place on a plate.

12 Serve with wild rice, corn (or your favorite vegetable), and the ginger chili sauce.

13 Sit back, relax, and enjoy!

PALE ALE MUSSELS

INGREDIENTS

- 4 lb mussels, sorted and cleaned
- 2 x 12 oz bottles American pale ale
- 1 x 28 oz can diced tomatoes
- ½ cup shallots, diced
- 6 cloves garlic, minced
- ⅓ cup fresh parsley, chopped
- 2 tbsp fresh thyme, chopped
- 3–4 tbsp red pepper flakes
- 2–3 tbsp olive oil
- ½ stick butter
- SPG seasoning, to taste
- French bread
- large Dutch oven

PITMASTER PRIVILEGE

You can increase the heat of this recipe to your liking—just adjust the quantities of the red pepper flakes.

For snacking or as a main meal these mussels are real good eating at the Pit.

METHOD

1 Bring grill temperature up to 375°F.

2 Sort and clean mussels, set aside.

3 Place Dutch oven directly over hot coals.

4 Add olive oil to pot and sauté shallots and garlic for a minute or two—do not overcook.

5 Pour in the can of diced tomatoes, parsley, thyme, and red pepper flakes. Add some SPG seasoning to taste, stir to combine well.

6 Add mussels to the pan and both bottles of pale ale and combine thoroughly.

7 Cover grill and simmer for 10–15 minutes, stirring halfway through cooking.

8 Mussels will be done when they open up.

9 Ladle mussels and broth into a large serving bowl.

10 Add butter and combine.

11 Serve with French bread to dip into the sauce.

12 Sit back, relax, and enjoy!

SCAN & WATCH

BBQ PIT BOYS

This is some guuud eatin'!

DRUNKEN CLAMS & SHRIMP

INGREDIENTS

- 4 lb little neck clams
- ¼ lb unsalted butter, divided
- 1 tbsp olive oil
- 2 green onion stalks, chopped
- 4–5 garlic cloves, crushed
- 2 cups white wine
- juice of 3 lemons
- 1 tsp red pepper flakes
- fresh ground black peppercorn, to taste
- ¼ lb 16/20 shrimp (easy peel, gutted, shell still on)
- French bread to dip

This classic clam dish is served with some shrimp and a wine and butter sauce!

METHOD

1 Heat olive oil and a little butter in a pan over flame.

2 Add green onion and garlic. Sauté briefly.

3 Add white wine and lemon juice.

4 Add the remaining butter and season with red pepper flakes and fresh ground black peppercorns. Stir and let it simmer.

5 Stir in clams and lay the shrimp right on top.

6 Cook until the shells open and shrimp is done, 4–5 minutes.

7 Serve hot with lemon wedges and French bread on the side.

SCAN & WATCH

BBQ PIT BOYS
It's about time to eat!

Get 'em drunk and they taste a whole lot better.

It smells Guuuuuud.....

SCAN & WATCH

SOUPS, SALADS & SIDES

WELCOME TO THE HEARTY WORLD OF SOUPS, SALADS, AND SIDES—BBQ PIT BOYS STYLE, WHERE EVERY DISH PACKS A FLAVORFUL PUNCH TO PERFECTLY COMPLEMENT YOUR BARBECUE FEAST.

SOUPS

These aren't just any soups; these are hearty blends of bold flavors, smoked and simmered to perfection.

SMOKE GRILLED ONION SOUP

This grilled onion soup recipe is an onion lover's classic. Smoked sweet onions gently simmered for a couple of hours in beef stock make it a barbecuing favorite side or main dish.

INGREDIENTS

- 4–5 lb large onions
- 14–16 cups beef stock
- 4 tbsp Worcestershire sauce
- olive oil/butter
- 12 oz beer
- 2–3 oz brandy or whiskey (optional)
- 2 tbsp mustard, pre-prepared
- salt, to taste
- toasted fresh bread or croutons
- grated cheese

METHOD

1 Slice onions at least ¼ inch thick.

2 Place a pan on the grill opposite the coals and add butter or olive oil to melt.

3 Coat the onion slices with butter/oil, then place them on the grill opposite the hot coals.

4 Add some of your favorite wood chunks or chips to the fire for a slight smoke.

5 Cover the grill, leave the onions to brown slightly—about 10–15 minutes. Then remove from the grill and chop into large chunks.

6 Put a deep pan on the grill, add the beef stock, the beer, and Worcestershire sauce.

7 Cover the grill and allow the soup to simmer slowly for about an hour or two.

8 Add salt, mustard, and brandy or whiskey, leave to simmer for another hour.

9 Serve with grated cheese on top and some fresh toasted bread or croutons.

SCAN & WATCH

BACON CHILI CORN CHOWDER

Grilled, fresh-shucked corn chowder is what good eating in the summer is all about!

INGREDIENTS

- ¾–1 lb bacon, thick sliced, cut into half-inch pieces (or smaller)
- 4 tbsp butter
- 1½–2 large onions, diced small
- 12 ears corn, shucked
- 4 whole chipotle peppers in adobo sauce
- 1 4–5 oz can diced green chilies, chopped
- 8 cups chicken broth
- 4 cups heavy cream
- 4–6 tbsp cornmeal, corn flour, or masa
- water

METHOD

1 Set the grill up for indirect cooking and place the bacon slices on the grill opposite the coals.

2 Rub some oil over the corn ears and place over the medium heat coals. Roast for 5 minutes and set aside.

3 Add butter and diced onion into a pot over the coals and stir, cooking for 3 to 4 minutes.

4 Chop the bacon, add to the pot, and cook for 2 minutes. Add both kinds of chilies and stir. Then pour in chicken broth. Stir and simmer for 20–25 minutes.

5 Shave the corn off the cobs and stir into the pan with the cream. Simmer for 20 minutes.

6 Add a little water to the cornmeal and stir to make a paste, then stir into the chowder. Cover and cook for 15–25 minutes over low heat.

7 If chowder needs more thickening, repeat step 6 but only cook for another ten minutes.

8 When it's ready, serve in a large soup bowl. Add some hot sauce if you want it hotter.

9 It's also great with oyster crackers or sourdough bread. Sit back, relax and enjoy!

BACON CHEESEBURGER SOUP

Make yourself some real cheeseburger soup made with grilled bacon cheeseburgers, beef stock and cheddar cheese.

INGREDIENTS

- 1 small onion, finely chopped
- 2–3 garlic cloves, minced
- 1 tbsp oil (as needed)
- 8 cups beef stock
- fresh ground black peppercorn, to taste
- 1 lb–1¼ lb cheddar cheese, shredded (or cheese of your choice)
- 2 tbsp milk (as needed)
- 6 bacon cheeseburgers (as needed), (see recipe page 19)
- salad vegetables to garnish (see opposite page)

METHOD

1 Heat the oil in a pan, sauté the onion and garlic for a couple of minutes.

2 Pour in beef stock, season with ground peppercorn, and bring to a simmer.

3 Add the shredded cheese and milk. Stir well, cover, and bring it back to simmer.

4 Break the bacon cheeseburgers into the pan and simmer for 10–15 minutes.

5 Serve hot with a selection of garnishes.

SCAN & WATCH

SCAN & WATCH

BACON & CHEDDAR POTATO SOUP

Bacon and cheddar cheese potato soup will surely cure what ails ya. So, fire up that grill!

INGREDIENTS

- 3 lb Yukon Gold potatoes, diced small
- ¼ lb bacon, smoked, grilled and chopped
- ½ lb cheddar cheese, shredded
- 4 tbsp butter
- oil or bacon fat (from previous cooking)
- 1 large onion, chopped
- approx. 8 cups chicken stock or broth
- ¼ cup cream or milk
- green onion to garnish
- SPG seasoning

METHOD

1 With the grill at 325°F, fry onions in butter over indirect heat (away from the coals).

2 Put the potatoes on a baking tray, pour bacon fat or oil over them, and sprinkle with SPG.

3 When done, take the onions off the grill and replace with the potatoes. Cover and cook for half an hour, until the outsides are just soft.

4 Put potatoes in a pot, add chicken stock to cover them, and add three slices of bacon and the onions.

5 Partially blend with a hand held blender, add cheese, and blend again. Add a little heavy cream or milk, blend again, and simmer.

6 Serve with some SPG, shredded cheese, bacon, and green onions.

GARNISHES

SALADS

Get ready to toss up some of the BBQ Pit Boys' favorite salads, where fresh, crisp greens meet a burst of intense flavor.

GRILLED POTATO SALAD

This delicious and easy to grill potato salad makes for the perfect barbecue side dish.

INGREDIENTS

- 3 lb golden potatoes
- ⅓ lb smoked bacon, chopped
- 2 eggs, hard boiled and chopped
- 2 tbsp parsley, finely chopped
- ¼ cup sweet onion
- salt and pepper, to taste

THE VINAIGRETTE

- ½ cup balsamic vinegar
- ½ cup extra virgin olive oil
- 1 tbsp dijon mustard
- 1 tbsp maple syrup
- 1 clove garlic, minced
- salt and pepper, to taste

METHOD

1 Set up your grill for indirect heat (hot coals on one side of the grill and no coals on the other side of the grill). You're looking for a grill temperature between 375°F–400°F.

2 Coat the potatoes with olive oil and place on the side of the grill with no coals.

3 Cover the grill with the lid with the top vent directly over the potatoes.

4 Cook for about 50 to 60 minutes.

5 In a jar or container that seals tightly, combine the balsamic vinegar, extra virgin olive oil, dijon mustard, maple syrup, minced garlic, salt, and pepper.

6 Seal the jar and shake to mix ingredients well.

7 After potatoes are done, remove them from the grill and let them cool down until just warm to the touch. This allows them to firm up, making them easier to cube.

8 When cool, cut the potatoes into bite sized cubes.

9 In a bowl combine the potatoes, bacon, onions, eggs, and parsley.

10 Shake the vinaigrette to mix and pour over the potato salad, stirring to coat the salad with the vinaigrette.

11 Serve and enjoy!

SCAN & WATCH

PINEAPPLE, CHICKEN & AVOCADO TOMATO SALAD

A recipe for the veggie-matics!

INGREDIENTS

- 4 boneless chicken breasts
- 1 head lettuce, chopped
- 2 avocados, chopped
- 1 large tomato, sliced, then quartered
- cherry tomatoes, halved
- 1 large sweet onion, sliced
- 1 lime, sliced
- 1 pineapple, peeled, sliced, and seared

FOR THE MARINADE

- ½ cup pineapple juice
- ¼ cup soy sauce
- 2 tbsp honey
- 1 tsp garlic, minced
- 1 tsp ginger, minced
- 2 green onions, chopped
- 2 tbsp cilantro, chopped
- juice of 1 lime

METHOD

1 Combine the marinade ingredients, reserving some. Pour into a resealable plastic bag, add the chicken, and marinate for 3–4 hours.

2 Sear chicken breasts over hot coals, then cook away from coals with lid on until done. Re-sear over hot coals briefly before serving.

3 Combine salad ingredients on a serving plate with the pineapple and chicken. Serve with warmed reserved marinade sauce.

BLACK BEAN SALAD

Beans, bacon, bell peppers, onions, celery, and a few spices make for some good eating, as shown with this classic barbecue beans dish.

INGREDIENTS

- 1 can each black beans and pinto beans
- ¼ lb bacon, thick cut, chopped
- ½ cup each red and green bell pepper, finely chopped
- ½ cup celery, finely chopped
- ½ cup sweet onion, finely chopped
- ½ cup fresh parsley, finely chopped
- good pinch kosher salt
- ¼–½ tsp Louisiana hot sauce
- 2 tbsp brown sugar
- 2 tbsp dijon mustard
- 2 tbsp apple cider vinegar
- 2 tbsp extra virgin olive oil

METHOD

1 Preheat grill to 350°F, with coals on one side for indirect cooking. Set a large cast iron skillet directly over coals to heat up.

2 Prepare the vegetables as described above.

3 Heat oil in the skillet, fry the bacon, then add the onions and cook 2–3 minutes until translucent.

4 Drain the beans into a colander and rinse with water.

5 Add the peppers and celery to the skillet and cook 2–3 minutes. Do not overcook.

6 Pour in the beans and mix together thoroughly. Remove from direct heat.

7 In skillet, combine the vinegar, mustard, and brown sugar. Add some salt and the hot sauce. Stir until well mixed.

8 Take the skillet off the grill. Allow it to cool to ambient temperature before serving.

9 Top with chopped parsley, stir into the salad, and serve with steak or pork chops.

10 Sit back, relax, and enjoy!

Our side dishes are good enough to be the star of the show, but they make perfect companions to any BBQ dish.

MAC AND CHEESE

This classic macaroni and cheese (and ham!) casserole is rib-stickin' good eatin' as a side dish, or as a main dish. And it's real easy to do!

INGREDIENTS

- 1 lb macaroni
- 16 cups water
- 2 tsp salt
- ½ cup breadcrumbs (or crumbled cheese flavored crackers)

MILK SAUCE

- 4 cups milk
- 6–8 green onion stalks
- 5–6 chili peppers
- ¾-inch piece sliced ham, water cured
- 3½ cups extra sharp cheddar cheese, grated, divided
- 1 cup pepper jack cheese, grated
- 3–4 slices pork belly bacon, chopped
- 3–4 tbsp flour
- 3–4 tbsp extra virgin olive oil

METHOD

1 Bring grill temperature up to 350°F. Place coals on one side for indirect cooking.

2 Bring water and salt to a boil. Add macaroni and cook only to al dente, strain well.

3 Add some SPG or other seasoning to taste.

4 Lightly coat chili peppers, green onions, and ham with oil. Place the vegetables over hot coals and ham to one side. Sear for 3–5 minutes then flip them to sear the other side.

5 After about 2 minutes, take peppers and green onions off the grill, move the ham closer to the coals and leave for a few more minutes.

6 Remove stems and some of the skin from the peppers. Remove root ends from the green onions. Chop peppers and green onions.

7 Take the ham off the grill and cut into ¾ inch pieces, then set aside.

8 Place a large cast iron pan (Dutch oven type) over the coals to heat up, and cook the bacon.

9 Move the pan to the opposite side of the grill for indirect heat, add the flour, and gradually stir in the milk. Do not boil, just heat until hot.

10 Add the cheeses (reserving some to top macaroni with), stirring until melted. Keep the sauce hot on the grill.

11 Stir in the ham, peppers, and green onions. Then add macaroni to the sauce and mix well.

12 Top the macaroni with the remainder of the cheddar and pepper jack cheeses.

13 Sprinkle breadcrumbs (or crackers if using) over the top of the cheese.

14 Cover the grill and let cook for 20 minutes, then rotate the pot, cover grill, and cook for a further 20 minutes.

15 After 40–45 minutes, when the mac and cheese is done, remove the pan from the grill.

16 Serve with smoked sausage links or natural casing hot dogs. Sit back, relax, and enjoy!

SCAN & WATCH

BLACK IRON POTATOES

Grilled potatoes, butter-roasted and then topped with bacon and shredded cheese, is not only GUUUD eating, but is real easy to do on a grill!

INGREDIENTS

- 10–12 small to medium potatoes—golden or yellow, peeled or unpeeled
- 1 large onion, chopped
- 2 cloves garlic, minced
- 1 stick butter
- 1 cup cheddar cheese, shredded (or your favorite cheese, shredded)
- 1 cup smoked bacon, chopped
- salt and pepper, to taste

METHOD

1 Set up the grill for in direct cooking, with hot coals on one side of the grill and no coals on the other side. Preheat to a temperature of about 400°F–450°F.

2 Place the onion, garlic, and stick of butter into a small iron skillet. Place the skillet on the side of the grill with no coals. You are not trying to cook the onions, just melt the butter.

3 Fill a large iron skillet with the whole potatoes. With a sharp knife, cut the potatoes into ¼ inch slices while they are in the pan. This makes it easier to handle the potatoes.

4 Season the potatoes with salt and pepper, then pour the butter, onions, and garlic over them. Place the skillet of potatoes on the indirect heat side of the grill.

5 Cover the grill with the lid (top vent over the potatoes) and cook for about an hour, depending on your grill temperature.

6 Top the potatoes with cheddar cheese and bacon, recover grill with the lid.

7 After a few minutes, when the cheese has melted, remove from the grill.

8 Serve and enjoy!

CANDIED BACON JALAPEÑO SMOKED CREAM CHEESE

Take your smoked cream cheese to the next level by adding candied bacon and jalapeños! You'll never do smoked cream cheese the plain way again.

INGREDIENTS

- 2 blocks cream cheese
- Sweet Martha, or your favorite rub
- Big Texan, or your favorite rub
- 4–5 strips of bacon
- 1 jalapeño pepper, cored and diced
- 4 tbsp brown sugar (or as needed)
- BBQ sauce, as needed
- honey, to drizzle

METHOD

1 Cover a baking pan with foil and place the cream cheese on the pan.

2 With a knife, score the top of the cream cheese in a cross hatch pattern about 1 inch apart.

3 Season the cream cheese with your favorite rub on all sides to cover.

4 Place in the smoker at 180°F for 2 hours.

5 Lay your bacon strips out and spread on some BBQ sauce.

6 Sprinkle bacon with your favorite BBQ rub, generously cover in brown sugar. Repeat on the other side.

7 Cook on another grill or oven at 325°F for about an hour or until crispy. Flip the bacon half way through. Then break the bacon up into a fine crumble.

8 After 2 hours remove the cream cheese from the smoker. Run some BBQ sauce in the gaps of the cross hatch that will now have opened up.

9 Continue smoking for another 45 minutes to let the BBQ sauce "tack" up.

10 When the cream cheese is done drizzle some honey over it and then sprinkle some of the crumbled bacon and diced jalapeños on top.

11 Serve with your favorite food shovel.

PITMASTER TIP

We recommend keeping some of the remaining crumbled bacon and jalapeños and set alongside the cream cheese so people can add as extra toppings as they wish.

SCAN & WATCH

CHIPOTLE SHRIMP STUFFED PEPPERS

Let's get a little cranked up over this one & check all the boxes in this delicious twist on your mom's old go-to fast dinner. It's so easy to do and it's GUUUD!!! Seafood check, chipotle check, veggies check, garlic check. All there, let's do it!

INGREDIENTS

- 7 garlic cloves, crushed
- ½ stick butter
- 2 lb medium shrimp, cleaned and chopped small
- ¼ cup fish sauce
- 1 tsp salt
- 1 tsp white pepper
- 2 tbsp corn starch
- 2 egg whites
- 1½ cups panko breadcrumbs
- 2 limes, 1 zested, 1 for juice
- ½ cup chipotle peppers
- 5 (or more) large red sweet bell peppers
- 2 lb shrimp, large, de-veined, with tail on

METHOD

1 In a Dutch-oven style pan over hot coals, sauté the garlic in the butter. Meanwhile, finely chop the shrimp.

2 Put the chopped shrimp into a large bowl. Add the fish sauce, salt, pepper, and corn starch—mix well with your fingers.

3 Add ½ cup panko breadcrumbs and mix well.

4 Pour the butter and garlic into the remaining panko.

5 Set up the Dutch oven pan over hot coals to a temperature of 300°F–325°F. Place some hot coals on the lid as this recipe requires heat from the top as well as the bottom.

6 Add the zest of 1 lime to the shrimp mixture, then add the butter, garlic and panko mixture. Combine thoroughly with your fingers.

7 Cut one end off each pepper and clean out the insides using scissors.

8 Stuff each pepper with the shrimp mixture and place some chipotle peppers into the top of each pepper.

9 Add a whole shrimp to the top of each pepper, place the peppers into the dutch oven pan, and cook for about 20–25 minutes.

10 Squeeze some lime juice on before eating if desired.

11 Eat and enjoy!

GRILLED JALAPEÑO POPPERS

Try these delicious and real easy to do jalapeño peppers, stuffed with romano and jack cheese, wrapped in bacon and grilled.

INGREDIENTS

- 6 fresh jalapeño peppers—the larger the better for stuffing.
- 1 onion, finely chopped/minced
- 1 cup romano cheese (or a sharp cheddar), shredded—the sharper the better, because it complements the heat of the jalapeños
- 1 cup jack cheese, shredded
- 1 pack bacon—a basic cut works great

PITMASTER TIP

Make sure you get plenty, because they are going to go fast!

METHOD

1 Slice open the jalapeños by cutting a side off—just cut off enough to open the pepper up so you can remove the seeds and white meat.

2 Scrape out the seeds and white meat into a bowl using the back side of a spoon. The real heat of the jalapeño comes from that white meat and not so much the seeds. We will add some of this white meat back into our cheese stuffing.

3 For the stuffing, add to a mixing bowl: the chopped onions, the shredded romano cheese (or your favorite cheese), the shredded jack cheese, and the jalapeño sides and meat you trimmed off and removed (be careful how much you use).

4 Mix all stuffing ingredients together well.

5 Cut the bacon in half—you will only need a half of slice per popper.

6 Stuff each popper pretty tightly with the cheese mixture.

SCAN & WATCH

7 After stuffing, wrap each jalapeño with a half slice of the bacon. If needed, you can use toothpicks to hold the bacon on.

8 Set up your grill for indirect cooking—hot coals all on one side of the grill and no coals on the other side.

9 Place your poppers on the side of the grill with no coals (indirect heat).

10 Cover, and in 15 to 20 minutes your poppers will be ready, depending on your grill temperature.

11 Place the poppers on a plate along with all your other favorite tailgating appetizers.

12 Serve and enjoy!

STRAWBERRY BACON JALAPEÑO POPPERS

These sweet, berry-stuffed, bacon wrapped jalapeños will change the game from the same ol' poppers you're serving up at your pit. Check out how easy it is to do this Martha fave.

INGREDIENTS

- 8 large jalapeños
- 12 oz plan cream cheese (about a box and a half)
- 16 slices bacon
- 4 cups fresh strawberries
- ¼ cup sugar

METHOD

1 Mash strawberries in a bowl.

2 Add sugar, and continue to mash until large chunks are gone and have a liquid texture.

3 Using a mixer, mix cream cheese and strawberries until smooth and well blended.

4 Core out jalapeños and cut tops off (these will be used later).

5 Pipe in the strawberry cream cheese mixture, put tops back on and secure with toothpick.

6 Wrap two slices of bacon on each of the poppers, securing with toothpicks.

7 Prepare the grill with temperature of 300°F–325°F and place poppers over indirect heat.

8 Cover and cook for about 45 minutes, flipping the poppers halfway through.

SCAN & WATCH

SWEET BACON CORNBREAD

Serving up cornbread is a must at any barbecue but this old-time sweet cornbread that's filled with fresh bacon will bring tears to a grown man's eyes!

INGREDIENTS

- ½ lb thick-sliced bacon
- 1 ¾ cups all purpose flour
- ¼ tsp baking soda
- 1 ½ tbsp baking powder
- 1 cup corn meal
- ¼ cup brown sugar
- ¼ cup cane sugar
- 1 pinch salt
- 2 tbsp butter
- 2 cups milk
- 1 tsp molasses
- 3 fresh eggs
- favorite corn bread toppings

SCAN &
WATCH

METHOD

1 Set up your grill for indirect heat—the grill temperature should be at 350°F.

2 Place your skillet on the grill over direct heat and put ½ lb of thick sliced bacon in it to cook—make sure to watch the bacon so it does not burn!

3 While bacon is cooking mix up your corn bread mix—for a better consistency, make a dry mix and a wet mix separately then combine them at the end.

4 Into one mixing bowl, combine all of the dry ingredients: the flour, baking soda, baking powder, corn meal, brown sugar, cane sugar, and salt.

5 In a separate mixing bowl combine the wet ingredients: the eggs, molasses, and milk.

6 Mix wet and dry mixes together by slowly adding the dry mix into the wet mix, whisking them together as you go. You are looking for the consistency of a light pancake batter. You may have to add more flour if it is too thin.

7 After bacon is cooked, remove from the skillet and place on a paper towel to remove excess grease.

8 Move the skillet adjacent to the coals for indirect heating and add butter to the bacon fat that is already in the skillet.

9 Cut up the bacon into ¼ to ½ inch pieces. Not too small—when you bite into that sweet corn bread you want a nice piece of bacon.

10 Pour corn bread mix into the skillet and then add the bacon into the mix.

11 Mix the bacon into the corn bread mix.

12 It will take 30 minutes to cook, depending on your grill temperature.

13 After 15 minutes, rotate the skillet so that you get an even cook on the corn bread.

14 At 30 minutes check for doneness with a toothpick. It should come out clean. Let sit 30 minutes before serving.

15 Serve with some eggs and home fries.

STUFFED CABBAGE IN HOT CHILI SAUCE

We do our version of the Golumpki AKA stuffed cabbage rolls. But no rice required!

INGREDIENTS

- 1 head of cabbage
- 9 large cabbage leaves
- 1 lb ground beef
- 1 lb ground pork
- 1 lb ground veal
- 2 eggs
- ½ cup beef stock
- ½ cup chopped onion
- 1 cup grated cauliflower
- 1 medium bell pepper, chopped
- 1 tsp lemon juice
- 1 tsp cider vinegar
- 1 tbsp SPG seasoning
- ½ cup brown sugar

CHILI SAUCE

- 2 cans tomato sauce
- ½ cup rice vinegar
- ½ cup dark brown sugar
- 1 tbsp minced garlic
- 1 tsp chili powder
- 2 tbsp minced onion
- ½ tsp red pepper flakes
- 1 cup water
- 1 tsp cayenne pepper
- 1 tsp corn starch
- 1 tbsp soy sauce

METHOD

1 In a saucepan, mix the tomato sauce, rice vinegar, brown sugar, minced garlic, onion, chili powder, red pepper flakes, water, cayenne pepper, corn starch, and the soy sauce. Stir over medium heat until all ingredients are dissolved, then set aside.

2 Remove the center core of the cabbage and place the head (core facing down) in a large pot with about two inches of water at the bottom and steam to release the leaves. It should take about 2 minutes per 4 leaves.

3 Add the bell pepper, onion, and the cauliflower together in an oil-coated frying pan and cook until the veggies are starting to soften.

4 In a bowl put the meat mixture, SPG, eggs, cider vinegar, lemon juice, brown sugar, beef stock, and the cooked pepper, onion, and cauliflower. Mix well.

5 Lay the cabbage leaves out. Scoop about 1½ tbsp of the mixture into each cabbage leaf, fold the sides in and roll the leaves into rolls.

6 Take a baking dish and coat the inside with oil, place the cabbage rolls into the pan, and pour the chili sauce over the cabbage until rolls are half covered.

7 Place pan over indirect heat on the grill at about 375°F for 45–60 minutes, depending on the roll size. Rotate pan halfway through for even cooking.

8 Sit back, relax, and enjoy!

SCAN &
WATCH

BACON STUFFING

SCAN & WATCH

Need a special holiday stuffing?
We've got you covered!

INGREDIENTS

- 1 lb thick bacon
- ¼ cup green onions, chopped
- ¼ cup celery, chopped
- 1 tbsp minced garlic
- juice of 1 lemon
- 2 tbsp parsley, finely chopped
- 2 boxes baked crackers, crushed
- ½ cup unsalted butter, melted
- salt and pepper, to taste
- 1 cup (or more) chicken broth
- 1 lb clams
- 1 lb shrimps

METHOD

1 Preheat grill to 350°F and cook bacon on indirect heat for about an hour. Place foil below bacon to collect bacon fat. Chop bacon and set aside.

2 Steam the clams in a pot until they open up. Take the meat out of the shell and chop.

3 Place the bacon, clams, garlic, celery, green onion, parsley, and crackers in a large bowl. Mix well and season with salt and pepper.

4 Pour melted butter into the bowl and gradually add the chicken broth to make the mixture moist.

5 Add the lemon juice and mix to combine. Set it aside.

6 Butterfly the shrimps (by making a shallow cut along their back), then place them on a baking tray along with the clam shells.

7 Stuff the clam shells and the slits in the shrimp with the bacon mixture, then place the tray on indirect heat to grill for about 25 minutes.

8 Remove from the grill and serve with the hot sauce of your choosing.

BREAD STUFFING

SCAN & WATCH

This bread stuffing deliciously accompanies
falling-off-the-bone tender spare ribs.

INGREDIENTS

- 8–10 cups seasoned breadcrumbs
- ¼ cup onion, diced
- 1 cup celery, diced
- 4 cups chicken broth
- pinch salt and black pepper

METHOD

1 Combine first four ingredients in a bowl.

2 Season, and stir well to combine.

LOBSTER & BRANDY STUFFING

SCAN & WATCH

Stuffed fish is good eating any time
of the year, especially when served
hot off the grill.

INGREDIENTS

- 3 green onions, sliced thinly
- 4–5 cloves garlic, minced
- 1 stick unsalted butter
- 2 packages Ritz crackers
- ¼ cup Italian-style breadcrumbs
- 4 lb lobster (or other seafood), cooked
- small bunch parsley, chopped
- ¼ cup brandy
- juice of 1 lemon

METHOD

1 Break open the lobster, remove the meat, and chop into fairly large chunks.

2 Melt butter in a pan and sauté the green onions and garlic. Then stir in the crackers, breadcrumbs, and lobster.

3 Add the lemon juice, brandy, and parsley. Warm thoroughly. Great stuffing for any fish recipe.

RELISH & SALSA

These relishes and salsas are the perfect blends of spice and freshness to complement your BBQ creations.

FIRE-ROASTED CHILI PEPPER RELISH

Take those burgers and dogs to the next level with this easy pepper relish: slow-roasted chili peppers with a tangy onion sauce.

INGREDIENTS

- 2–3 lb chili peppers (poblanos, serranos, jalapeños; whatever is available)
- 1 large onion, sliced ½ inch thick
- ½ cup brown sugar
- ½ cup dijon mustard
- 2–3 tbsp apple cider vinegar
- salad oil or olive oil
- salt and pepper, to taste

METHOD

1 Put the whole chilis in a large bowl, pour some salad oil on the peppers, and turn the peppers in the oil to coat them.

2 Place the peppers over the coals of a medium temperature grill, about 300°F, to sear.

3 After 4–5 minutes, flip the peppers. Place the onions on the grill opposite the coals, and drizzle with oil. Cover and cook.

4 Remove the peppers when done, put them in a large bowl, and cover with plastic wrap for 5–10 minutes, making them easier to peel.

5 Roughly skin and de-seed the peppers and place them in a new bowl.

6 Take onions off the grill and chop roughly. Place them in the pepper bowl. Add the brown sugar, dijon mustard, and apple cider vinegar, stir, and serve on a burger or with any grilled dish.

GRILLED CORN SALSA

Here we show you how to grill whole trout, and then serve it with this fabulous grilled corn salsa.

INGREDIENTS

- 3 firm tomatoes, halved
- 1 onion, halved
- 1 tbsp olive oil, divided (as needed)
- 2 jalapeño peppers
- juice of 1 lemon
- salt and pepper, to taste
- 1 tbsp cilantro, chopped (as needed)
- 1 corn on the cob, cooked
- 1 tsp garlic, minced (as needed)

METHOD

1 Preheat grill to 325°F.

2 Coat tomato halves, onion, and jalapeños peppers with olive oil and place them on the grill, over indirect heat.

3 Cover and cook for 15 minutes.

4 Remove tomato, onion, and jalapeños from the grill. Peel the tomatoes and onion and chop finely, removing the tomato core at the same time. Place them in a bowl.

5 Chop the jalapeños finely and place them in the bowl.

6 Add lemon juice, salt, pepper, a little olive oil, and cilantro. Mix well.

7 Cut the kernels off the corn cob—hold the cob vertically, slicing downward.

8 Add the corn to your salsa. Mix and set aside. Add the garlic just before serving.

SAUCES, GRAVIES, RUBS & MARINADES

SAUCES, GRAVIES, RUBS, AND MARINADES ARE WHERE THE MAGIC REALLY HAPPENS. THESE RECIPES PROVIDE THE ESSENTIAL FLAVORS THAT TRANSFORM GOOD MEAT INTO GREAT BARBECUE. EACH RECIPE PACKED WITH THE BOLD, SMOKY, AND SAVORY TASTES THAT DEFINE OUR STYLE.

SAUCES

These bold signature sauces will turn any meal into a BBQ Pit Boys classic.

LIQUID GOLD BBQ SAUCE

This liquid gold BBQ sauce will blow your mind. Grill up some country ribs and chicken, and give it the liquid gold sauce treatment.

INGREDIENTS

- 1½ lb unsalted butter
- 3 lb light brown sugar
- 1 lb white cane sugar
- 10 cups yellow mustard
- 2 cups apple cider vinegar
- 2 tbsp red pepper flakes
- 1 tbsp fresh ground black peppercorns

METHOD

1 Melt the butter in a large saucepan over medium to low heat. Add the sugars and dissolve into the butter, stirring regularly so it doesn't burn.

2 Add the mustard, apple cider vinegar, red pepper flakes and pepper, and stir.

3 Let the sauce simmer, stirring often until desired thickness is reached.

4 Enjoy!

SCAN & WATCH

SCAN & WATCH

VODKA BBQ SAUCE

Looking for a homemade BBQ sauce for dippin' in? Try this vodka sauce for a flavor that is second to none. All you need is some vodka and a few basic spices. Its thick and hearty tomato-base goes well with most anything "barbecue." We always make a double batch of this recipe so we can keep a jar handy in the refrigerator.

INGREDIENTS

- 4 cups ketchup
- 1 cup apple cider vinegar
- 1 tbsp ground cumin
- ½ tbsp garlic powder
- 1 tbsp chili powder
- 1 tbsp cayenne pepper
- juice of 1 lemon
- ¼ cup sugar
- ⅛ cup salt
- 1 cup vodka

METHOD

1 In a pan, combine together all ingredients, stirring until well mixed.

2 Simmer over the coals for about 20 minutes.

ALABAMA WHITE SAUCE

On chicken, on pork, or on burgers, this classic BBQ sauce has been a favorite for over 40 years for Pitmasters worldwide. And for good reason. You can use it as a marinade, to baste, and as a dipping sauce.

INGREDIENTS

- 2 cups mayonnaise
- ¼ cup extra hot prepared horseradish
- 2 tsp yellow mustard
- 2 tbsp apple cider vinegar
- 1½ tsp ground black peppercorns
- 1 tsp kosher salt
- 1 tsp cayenne pepper
- 1 tsp garlic powder
- ½ lemon

METHOD

1 Combine the black pepper, kosher salt, cayenne pepper and garlic powder.

2 Put the mayonnaise, horseradish, mustard, and apple cider vinegar in a large bowl.

3 Add the spice mixture to the bowl.

4 Squeeze half a lemon into the bowl and mix well.

5 Your Alabama white sauce is ready to use.

SCAN & WATCH

CLAM SAUCE

This recipe goes real well with pork ribs, beef, and chicken.

INGREDIENTS

- 1 lb clams, in shell
- 1 clove garlic, crushed
- 1 shallot, finely diced
- 2 tbsp lemon juice
- 1 stick butter
- 1 cup chopped clams
- 1 cup white wine
- ½–¾ cup heavy cream

METHOD

1 Place a skillet on the grill over the hot coals.

2 Melt 1 tbsp of butter in the pan. Add the diced shallot and the crushed garlic to the pan to sweat.

3 Add the white wine, more butter, and the lemon juice.

4 Add the clams to the skillet, cover the grill with the lid, and cook until the clams have opened.

5 Pour the heavy cream and the chopped clams into the skillet.

6 Move the skillet to the side of the grill with no coals.

7 Cover the grill with the lid, allowing the sauce to simmer gently and reduce.

8 Use as desired.

SCAN & WATCH

SCAN & WATCH

ORANGE GINGER BBQ SAUCE

This quick-and-easy barbecue sauce is the perfect brush-on for beef, chicken, pork, and poultry.

INGREDIENTS

- 1 cup BBQ sauce
- ½ cup orange juice concentrate
- 4 tbsp soy sauce
- ½ tsp hot sauce
- 2 tbsp fresh ginger, grated

METHOD

1 Set up your grill for indirect heat (hot coals on one side of the grill and no coals on the other side of the grill).

2 Place your pot directly over the hot coals.

3 Add all of the ingredients to the pot in the order listed.

4 Stir to combine the ingredients. Simmer for five minutes, stirring occasionally to prevent the sauce from burning.

5 This sauce can be brushed on your favorite meat about 5 minutes before it's ready to come off the grill, and is also good as a dipping sauce.

CHILI BEER BBQ SAUCE

A quick and simple barbecue sauce you can't buy off the shelf. It goes great with beef, pork, and poultry, so be sure to make a big batch!

INGREDIENTS

SCAN & WATCH

- cooking oil
- 2 cloves of garlic, chopped
- 1 cup onions, chopped
- 2 cups of chili sauce
- ½ cup of honey
- 4 tbsp of Worcestershire sauce
- 2 tbsp of prepared mustard
- hot sauce, to taste
- 12 oz of beer

METHOD

1 Set the grill up for indirect cooking. Heat the oil in a pan over the hot coals.

2 Add the onions and garlic and sauté for a couple of minutes to soften.

3 Add the chili sauce and honey. Stir the mixture so it doesn't burn.

4 Add the remaining ingredients, stir well, then simmer to thicken the sauce for 20 minutes.

5 Brush the sauce thickly onto any meat 10–15 minutes before it's finished cooking.

INDEPENDENCE DAY HELL FIRE HOT SAUCE

We salute all those who fought for freedom with this roasted pepper hell fire barbecue sauce.

INGREDIENTS

- 40 habanero peppers
- 4 serrano chili peppers
- 2–3 jalapeño peppers
- 3–4 tbsp olive oil
- 10–12 garlic cloves
- 1 cup water
- 1 cup distilled white vinegar
- ½ cup lemon juice
- 2 tbsp molasses
- 1 tbsp smoked paprika
- 1 tsp kosher salt
- 2 tbsp hot pepper sauce

METHOD

1 Bring grill temperature up to 300°F. Place coals on one side for indirect cooking.

2 Slice the habanero peppers and remove seeds and membrane. *"Do NOT rub your eyes or scratch your Boys, if you know what I mean!"* Gloves are recommended for handling the habaneros as the juice WILL burn your skin.

3 Slice the remaining peppers, then remove and discard the seeds and membrane.

4 Coat the bottom of a baking pan with olive oil. Place the peppers in the pan, turning them to coat with the olive oil.

5 Add the garlic to the pan.

6 Place the baking pan on the grill over indirect heat, cover with the lid and cook for 20–25 minutes.

7 Thoroughly wash hands, utensils, and cooking areas with soap and water to remove pepper juices.

8 Remove pan from grill and place peppers and garlic in a blender.

9 Add the water, vinegar, lemon juice, molasses, smoked paprika, salt, into the hot pepper sauce, and blend thoroughly.

10 Carefully pour into mason jars and secure the lids tightly. Use to baste ribs, chicken, burgers, rice, or anything that needs a little kick—either on the grill or in the smoker.

SCAN & WATCH

BOURBON BBQ SAUCE

A tangy tomato, vinegar, mustard, and bourbon whiskey-based barbecue sauce that's the perfect match for grilled chicken, beef, and pork.

INGREDIENTS

SCAN & WATCH

- 2 cups ketchup
- ½ cup lemon juice
- 4 tbsp brown sugar
- 4 tbsp apple cider vinegar
- 2 tbsp Worcestershire sauce
- 2 tsp mustard powder
- 1 tsp onion powder
- 1 tsp garlic powder
- 4 tbsp honey
- 1 cup bourbon

METHOD

1 Set up the grill for indirect cooking.

2 Put all of the ingredients in a pan over low to medium hot coals and stir to combine.

3 Add some smoke wood to the coals for that rich smoky flavor.

4 Bring the sauce to simmer, stirring. Move off the coals and cook on indirect heat for about five minutes to thicken.

5 Occasionally check and stir the sauce.

6 Once it's ready, use for basting your "low and slow" barbecue meat, or as a table sauce.

JALAPEÑO BEER BBQ SAUCE

A thick, buttery sauce that's quick and easy to make and goes real well with hot wings, chicken thighs, and drumsticks.

INGREDIENTS

SCAN & WATCH

- 4 cups ketchup
- 1 cup apple cider vinegar
- 1 tbsp garlic powder
- 1 tbsp cayenne powder
- 1 tbsp chili powder
- ¼ cup brown sugar
- 4 tbsp Worcestershire sauce
- 4 tbsp coarse salt
- 1 beer (8–12 oz)
- 3–4 jalapeño peppers, fresh or pickled, chopped
- 1 to 2 sticks butter

METHOD

1 In a pan over hot coals, add all the ingredients except the butter. Stir thoroughly to combine.

2 Break the butter into the sauce. Simmer until the sauce is thickened.

SCAN & WATCH

BBQ SAUCE COUNTRY STYLE

This thick and tasty tomato-based barbecue sauce recipe, is perfect for both dipping and mopping. It tastes real good on chicken, ribs, beef, and pork. Adjust the selection of spices and quantities to make it your own secret sauce!

INGREDIENTS

- 8 cups ketchup
- 2 cups apple cider vinegar
- ½ cup sugar
- 1–2 tbsp garlic powder
- 1 tbsp celery seed
- 1 tbsp ground cumin
- 1 tbsp chili powder
- 1–2 tbsp cayenne powder
- ⅛ cup coarse salt
- ½–1 cup water

METHOD

1 Mix all ingredients together, and then simmer on the grill for 5 minutes to thicken.

2 Depending on how thick you like your barbecue sauce, you can simmer for longer.

JALAPEÑO HONEY BBQ SAUCE

If you're looking for a go-to sticky, sweet heat sauce this is the one for you! It's guuud for basting, dipping, even as a base for bean or meat chili. Great on chicken, ribs, beef, or pork!

INGREDIENTS

SCAN & WATCH

- 4 cups ketchup
- 1½ cups dark brown sugar
- ½ cup apple cider vinegar
- ½ cup Worcestershire sauce
- 1 cup honey
- 1 tbsp garlic powder
- 1 tbsp onion powder
- 1 tbsp ground black pepper
- 1 x 7 oz can pickled jalapeño peppers

METHOD

1 In a pan on the grill, stir together the ingredients, cover, and simmer for 20 minutes.

2 Pour the sauce into a blender and blend until smooth.

3 Pour the sauce into jars to store. If you can keep your hands off it, it will keep for about three weeks refrigerated.

BABY SWEET COKE BBQ SAUCE

Oh, baby... it doesn't get any sweeter than this! This cola and brown sugar BBQ sauce will bring a smile to your sweet baby for sure.

INGREDIENTS

- 3 cups ketchup
- 2 cups chili sauce
- 2–4 tbsp black pepper, to taste
- 1 tbsp cinnamon
- 1 tbsp oregano
- 1 cup brown sugar
- 2 cups Coca-Cola
- 2 tbsp prepared mustard

METHOD

1 Set up your grill for indirect heat (hot coals on one side of the grill and no coals on the other side of the grill).

2 Place a pot on the side of the grill with no coals and add the ketchup, chili sauce, black pepper, cinnamon, oregano, and brown sugar.

3 Stir the sauce so the brown sugar dissolves and to prevent the sauce from burning.

4 Add the mustard, then gradually add the Coca-Cola, stirring all the time. Move the pot to sit over the hot coals.

5 Stir continually to mix ingredients and prevent the sauce from burning.

6 Move the sauce off the hot coals and cook for 10 minutes to thicken.

7 Brush this sweet barbecue sauce onto your favorite meat about 10 minutes before it is ready to come off the grill.

8 Serve and enjoy!

MINT SAUCE

You won't believe how good this is with roast lamb, mashed potatoes, peas, and gravy!

INGREDIENTS

- 1 bunch fresh mint
- ½ tbsp salt
- 1 tbsp sugar
- 8 tbsp boiling water
- 4 tbsp white wine or brown (malt) vinegar

METHOD

1 Strip off the mint leaves, sprinkle with the salt, and chop finely.

2 Place the chopped mint and salt into a bowl, add the sugar, and pour over the boiling water. Stir until dissolved and let it cool.

3 When cooled, stir in the vinegar, taste, and add more water or vinegar as required.

SCAN & WATCH

SCAN & WATCH

CIGAR ASH BBQ SAUCE

The ash of a fine cigar is mostly inert carbon and potassium. The potassium allows the sauce to thicken quickly and foam a bit...and the cigar was worth every toke.

INGREDIENTS

- ash from one large, good quality cigar
- 2 bottles of your favorite BBQ sauce
- 1 tsp apple cider vinegar
- 1 tsp apple juice
- SPG seasoning (or your favorite seasoning)

METHOD

1 Mix together in a pan on the grill the cigar ash, BBQ sauce, apple cider vinegar, and apple juice, until well blended.

2 Simmer to thicken over medium to low heat.

3 Add some SPG to taste and simmer until the sauce reaches your desired thickness.

KANSAS CITY BBQ SAUCE

If you like sticky sweet BBQ pork ribs then check out this thick, reddish-brown, tomato- and ketchup-based sauce.

INGREDIENTS

- 1 tbsp cooking oil
- 1 onion, chopped
- 4 cups chicken broth
- 1½ cups cola
- 1 cup apple cider vinegar
- 1 cup dark corn syrup
- 1 cup molasses
- ½ cup ketchup
- ½ cup tomato paste
- ½ tsp garlic powder
- 2–3 tbsp brown mustard
- hot sauce, to taste

METHOD

1 Heat the oil in a pan, add the onion, and cook until just soft.

2 Then add one by one, all the ingredients in the order listed above.

3 Stir to mix and leave it to cook and thicken for about an hour.

4 Use with your favorite barbecued meats.

SCAN & WATCH

Try our favorite gravies to add the perfect finishing touch to your BBQ dishes.

SCAN & WATCH

MEAT GRAVY

This is all about the gravy! And it's perfect for a roast beef sub sandwich and as a sauce over mashed potatoes!

INGREDIENTS

- 1 lb roast beef, thinly sliced and chopped
- ⅛ lb good butter
- 1 tsp SPG seasoning
- ½ cup all purpose flour
- 4 cups beef stock
- 1 tbsp cayenne pepper

METHOD

1 Melt the butter in a pan and season with SPG.

2 Add the flour and stir until it's completely blended into the butter. Stir in half of the chopped roast beef.

3 Slowly stir in the beef stock until blended in.

4 Add the rest of the chopped beef to the gravy.

5 Move off the hot coals and slowly simmer to thicken up. It's ready to use as you choose!

STEAK & BOURBON GRAVY

This gravy goes real well with steak and taters!

INGREDIENTS

- 3–4 slices bacon, chopped
- 1 tbsp cooking oil
- 1 stick butter
- ½–¾ cup onions, diced
- ½ lb mushrooms, sliced
- 1 tbsp all-purpose flour
- salt and black pepper, to taste
- ½ cup bourbon
- 20 cups beef stock
- 1 piece sirloin steak

METHOD

1 Heat the oil in a pan and add the bacon. After a few minutes, add the butter, stir as it melts.

2 Add the onions and mushrooms, season with salt and pepper. Simmer.

3 Stir in the bourbon. Add the flour and stir as it makes a paste. Then stir in the beef stock and let it simmer away from the hot coals.

4 Cook the steak over the coals until it's medium-rare, then chop into small pieces. Add to the gravy and simmer for 15–20 minutes.

SCAN & WATCH

ONION GRAVY

If you like pork chops you gotta check out this onion gravy! It's a match made in Heaven!

INGREDIENTS

- 1 medium onion, diced
- 3 garlic cloves, chopped
- ¼ cup butter
- Italian seasoning, to taste
- 1 tbsp flour
- 4 cups chicken stock
- salt and pepper, to taste

METHOD

1 Preheat grill.

2 In a heated pan, place onion, garlic and butter, sauté for few seconds.

3 Add Italian seasoning and flour, stirring constantly.

4 When slightly cooked, gradually add chicken stock, stirring all the time until the stock has been absorbed.

5 Simmer for few minutes, season with salt and pepper, and serve warm with grilled pork chops.

BACON & SCALLION CRÈME GRAVY

This gravy goes real well with pork and chicken, particularly chicken cordon bleu.

INGREDIENTS

- 2 slices of bacon, diced
- 1 tbsp oil
- 4 tbsp butter
- 3 tbsp all-purpose flour
- 6 cups beef or chicken broth
- ¾ cup of heavy cream
- 2–3 bunches of green onion, chopped

METHOD

1 Heat oil in a pan over direct heat on the grill, then add the butter. Stir as it melts.

2 Add the diced bacon and fry until just brown.

3 Add the flour, whisking as the gravy thickens.

4 Stir in the stock, followed by the cream.

5 Once the sauce has thickened up, move to indirect heat to simmer for a few minutes.

6 Serve warm, poured over the meat of your choice, and scatter the green onions over the top.

RUBS & SEASONINGS

A good rub or marinade is at the heart of guuud grillin'.
The following pages feature some of our favorites.

SCAN & WATCH

COUNTRY STYLE RIB RUB

This classic BBQ dry rub recipe for barbecue ribs is quick and simple to make. Use our formula, and then adjust the spices and quantities to make it your own! That's what barbecue and good eating is all about.

INGREDIENTS

- 3 tbsp coarse salt
- ¼ cup sugar
- ¼ cup brown sugar
- ¼ cup paprika
- 1 tbsp garlic powder
- 1 tbsp onion powder
- 1 tbsp chili powder
- 1 tbsp cayenne pepper powder
- 1 tbsp fresh ground black pepper

METHOD

1 Mix all the ingredients together with your fingers.

2 Store the rub in a jar or a resealable plastic bag until required.

SCAN & WATCH

MUD RUB

A specially created rub recipe for pork ribs, pork shoulders, Boston butts, loins, and chops.

INGREDIENTS

- ½ cup brown sugar
- 3 tbsp coarse salt
- 1 tbsp black pepper
- 2 tbsp paprika
- 2 tsp garlic powder
- 2 tsp cumin
- 1 tsp onion powder
- 1 tsp cayenne pepper
- 6 tbsp olive oil

METHOD

1 Thoroughly mix together all the dry ingredients with your fingers.

2 Add the oil and stir in.

3 Mix all ingredients with oil until it looks and feels like mud, and then apply to pat-dried ribs.

COFFEE DRY RUB

Check out this traditional coffee flavored barbecue rub. It's easy to make, and goes real good with poultry.

INGREDIENTS

SCAN & WATCH

- 6 tbsp ground coffee
- 2 tbsp brown sugar
- 2 tbsp coarse salt
- 2 tbsp sweet paprika
- 2 tbsp fresh ground pepper
- 2 tsp garlic powder
- 2 tsp onion powder
- 1 tsp ground coriander
- 2 tsp white sugar

METHOD

1 Mix all ingredients together with your hands.

2 Store in a resealable bag until needed.

SCAN & WATCH

KANSAS CITY DRY RUB

This classic Kansas City dry rub is not only easy to make, but is simply the perfect rub for most anything barbecue.

SCAN & WATCH

INGREDIENTS

- 2 cups sugar
- ½ cup coarse salt
- ¼ cup paprika (sweet or hot)
- 2 tsp chili powder
- ½ tsp cayenne pepper
- 1 tsp garlic powder
- 2 tsp coarse pepper

METHOD

1 Combine all ingredients with a whisk. Add more cayenne pepper for more heat.

2 Store the rub in a jar or a resealable plastic bag until required.

CHILI RUB

An all-purpose rub that's the perfect blend for poultry, beef, lamb, pork, and fish.

INGREDIENTS

- 8 tbsp coarse salt
- 8 tbsp paprika
- 4 tbsp brown sugar (light or dark brown)
- 6 tbsp chili powder
- 2 tsp ground cumin
- 1 tsp cayenne pepper (optional)
- 1 tbsp fresh ground black pepper

METHOD

1 Mix all ingredients with your fingers. If you want more heat, add cayenne pepper.

2 Store the rub in a jar or a resealable plastic bag until required.

HOMEMADE SPG

Make our famous SPG mix at home! You can enhance your favorite tastes by simply adjusting the quantities used.

INGREDIENTS

- 3 tbsp coarse salt
- 3 tbsp fresh ground black pepper
- 3 tbsp garlic powder

METHOD

1 Put all ingredients into a bowl and mix together with your fingers.

2 Store in a resealable bag, ready for your next barbecue!

CLASSIC AMERICAN RUB

Check out this classic American brown sugar dry rub. It's not only easy to make, but simply the perfect rub for most anything barbecue.

INGREDIENTS

- ½ cup brown sugar
- 4 tbsp coarse salt
- ¼ cup paprika
- 2 tsp celery seed
- 3 tbsp fresh ground black pepper
- 1 tsp cayenne pepper
- 2 tsp garlic powder
- 2 tsp onion powder

METHOD

1 Put all ingredients into a bowl.

2 Mix together with your hands, breaking up the moist sugar lumps as you go.

3 Add some cayenne pepper for additional heat if you want.

4 Store in a resealable bag, ready for the next time you fire up the barbecue!

DRY RUB FOR RIBS

This classic BBQ dry rub recipe for barbecue ribs is quick and simple to make. Use this recipe, and then adjust the spices and quantities to match your preferences.

INGREDIENTS

- ¼ cup sugar
- ¼ cup brown sugar
- ¼ cup paprika
- 3 tbsp coarse salt
- 1 tbsp black pepper
- 1 tbsp garlic powder
- 1 tbsp onion powder
- 1 tbsp chili powder (optional)
- 1 tbsp cayenne pepper (optional)

METHOD

1 Mix all the ingredients together with your fingers to break up any clumps of brown sugar.

2 Store in a resealable plastic bag, sealable bowl or a shaker bottle.

CAJUN DRY RUB

Check out this traditional barbecue rub if you love that deep south Cajun flavor. Easy to make, and real good with pork, chicken and fish.

SCAN & WATCH

INGREDIENTS

- ¼ cup coarse salt
- ¼ cup sweet paprika
- 1 tbsp garlic flakes (or granulated)
- 1 tbsp onion powder
- 1 tbsp dried thyme
- 1 tbsp dried oregano
- 2–3 tsp cayenne pepper, to taste
- 1 tbsp ground black pepper
- 1 tsp ground bay leaf

METHOD

1 Combine all ingredients into a bowl and mix with your fingers. Add more cayenne pepper for additional heat.

2 Rub on your favorite meat and let stand for an hour for maximum flavor.

PEPPER RUB

This easy to make BBQ dry rub is all about pepper. It goes real well with pork, chicken, and beef.

SCAN & WATCH

INGREDIENTS

- 3 tbsp coarse salt
- 3 tbsp fresh ground black pepper
- 3 tbsp red pepper flakes
- 3 tbsp onion flakes (or granulated)
- 3 tbsp dried parsley

METHOD

1 Put all ingredients into a bowl.

2 Mix together with your fingers.

3 Store in a resealable bag, ready for your next barbecue!

MARINADES

A good rub or marinade is at the heart of guuud grillin'. The following pages feature some of our favorites.

TENDER & MOIST PORK MARINADE

Check out this pork barbecue marinade and basting sauce for the grill. It's an easy recipe to make, and it also works real well with chicken and beef.

INGREDIENTS

- ¼ cup molasses
- ½ cup olive oil
- 1 tbsp red pepper flakes
- ¼ cup Worcestershire sauce
- 1 tbsp fresh ground black peppercorn
- 1–2 tsp garlic powder
- 1 tsp SPG seasoning
- ½ cup brown sugar
- 4 oz beer (your favorite)

METHOD

1 One by one add all ingredients to a pan, constantly stirring to combine. Your basting marinade sauce is ready to use!

2 Baste meat several times while cooking.

BEEF JERKY MARINADE

Perhaps the #1 working man's snack in the world, smoke dried beef is real easy to do on the grill or smoker. This is not your typical convenience store jerky.

SCAN & WATCH

INGREDIENTS

- 1 tbsp onion powder
- 1 tbsp garlic powder
- 1 tbsp red pepper flakes (optional)
- 1 tbsp fresh ground black peppercorns
- 1½ cups soy sauce
- 1½ cups Worcestershire sauce
- 5 lb steak, thinly sliced

METHOD

1 Combine all ingredients in a bowl.

2 Marinate steak for several hours in the marinade. For maximum flavor, up to 24 hours.

3 Dry the beef on paper towels and grill at 150°F max, off the coals, for 6 hours. Or smoke them without any water in the pan.

SCAN & WATCH

MARGARITA MARINADE (FOR RIBS)

Grilled half-cut pork spare ribs, marinated in a tequila, lime, and triple sec brine, makes what we call margarita ribs.

INGREDIENTS

- 1 cup water
- 1 cup tequila
- juice of 2 limes
- 4 tbsp triple sec liqueur
- 4 tbsp coarse salt
- 2 tbsp table sugar
- 1 tbsp cayenne pepper (use two for a hot marinade)
- 1 tbsp orange rind

METHOD

1 Combine all of the ingredients in a bowl or a releasable plastic bag.

2 Marinade your favorite meat in it for several hours for maximum flavor.

CHAIRMAN GOOSE MARINADE (FOR WILD GOOSE BREAST)

This marinade is perfect for wild goose, but it works great on any poultry.

INGREDIENTS

- 1½ tbsp pickled ginger
- 4 tbsp sweet & sour sauce
- 2 tbsp ponzu sauce
- 2 tbsp toasted sesame seeds
- 4 tbsp Worcestershire sauce
- 2½ tbsp sriracha sauce
- 1½ tbsp Emeril's Asian Essence

METHOD

1 Put all ingredients in a resealable plastic bag and seal the bag.

2 Turn the bag over and over in your hands to thoroughly mix the ingredients together.

3 Place each tenderized breast in the marinade and mix.

4 Let marinate 12–24 hours in the refrigerator or cooler.

ORANGE CHILI CHICKEN MARINADE

Not into turkey for the upcoming Thanksgiving holiday? Then you just gotta try this grilled orange chili chicken recipe... It's GUUUD!

INGREDIENTS

- SPG seasoning
- 4 oranges, halved for juice
- 1–1¼ cups sweet chili sauce
- orange juice (enough to cover chicken in the bag)

METHOD

1 Put the chickens into a resealable bag.

2 Season with SPG and then add the remaining ingredients.

3 Seal the bag, then turn over several times to combine the marinade and cover the chicken. Allow to marinade for 4–6 hours (or overnight) in the refrigerator.

SCAN & WATCH

BEER & CHILI MARINADE

A thick, buttery sauce that's quick and easy to make and goes real well with hot wings, chicken thighs, and legs.

INGREDIENTS

- 1 tbsp dry mustard
- 1 x 12 oz bottle chili sauce
- ½ cup green onion, chopped
- 12 oz beer (your favorite)
- 2 tbsp hot sauce
- 3–4 garlic cloves, crushed
- 1 jalapeño pepper, chopped

METHOD

1 Put all ingredients in a large resealable plastic bag, then close the bag securely.

2 Turn and knead the bag to thoroughly mix the ingredients together.

3 Place your prepared meat of choice in the bag with the sauce and allow to marinade for at least two hours. Longer is better.

MARINADE FOR STEAK

This quick and easy steak marinade is full of rich flavor, and it makes a perfect partner to our London broil recipe.

INGREDIENTS

- 12–16 oz beer
- ½ cup olive oil
- 1 tsp cayenne pepper
- 1 tbsp garlic powder
- 1 tbsp onion powder
- 2 tbsp Worcestershire sauce
- 1 tbsp ground pepper
- 1 tbsp prepared horseradish
- juice of ½ lemon

METHOD

1 Place 2 steaks in a resealable plastic bag.

2 Pour the marinade into the bag.

3 Seal and knead the bag to cover each steak.

4 Place the steak in the refrigerator for 4 to 24 hours.

ASIAN MARINADE

In this recipe we show you how to prepare this easy-to-make classic Asian dish on the grill.

INGREDIENTS

- ½ cup hoisin sauce
- ½ cup oyster sauce
- ½ cup soy sauce
- 4 tbsp garlic, minced
- ½–1 tsp cayenne pepper

METHOD

1 Place the marinade ingredients in a bowl, mix well, and allow to stand.

2 Add the meat—pork spare ribs work really well with this marinade—but other meats and poultry are great too.

SCAN & WATCH

DESSERTS

WE CAN DO CONVENTIONAL, LIKE SAY, BLACKBERRY RHUBARB PIE, OR GRANDMA'S GRILLED APPLE PIE, BUT WHY HAVE CINNAMON PUMPKIN PIE AND NOT ADD SOME WHISKEY? THROW SOME BACON INTO THE MIX, AND NOW YOU'RE DOIN' DESSERTS PIT BOY STYLE!

SCAN & WATCH

Oh me, oh my!

CINNAMON WHISKEY PUMPKIN PIE

INGREDIENTS

FOR THE PIE CRUST

- 2 x 9-inch frozen pie crusts (or make your own)

FOR THE PIE FILLING

- 1 x 30 oz can pure pumpkin
- 1 ½ cans (18 oz) evaporated milk
- 4 eggs
- 1½ cups sugar
- 1 tsp salt
- 1 tsp ground ginger
- ½ tsp ground cloves
- 6 oz Fireball cinnamon whiskey

Fireball cinnamon whiskey pumpkin pie is the perfect dessert for that holiday barbecue you have going on at your Pit.

METHOD

1 Bring grill temperature up to 400°F.

2 If using frozen pie crusts, follow the directions on the package and lay the dough into the base of oven-proof dishes.

3 Using a fork, poke small holes all over pie crust base.

4 Place pie crusts on grill opposite hot coals for 15–20 minutes. Cover grill.

5 Be sure to follow cooking times on the package of your frozen pie crusts.

6 Remove crusts from the grill and reduce heat to 325°F.

7 Crack eggs into a mixing bowl. Add the sugar, salt, ginger, cloves, pumpkin, evaporated milk, and cinnamon whiskey.

8 Whisk to thoroughly combine everything, then divide the mixture between each pie crust.

9 When the grill reaches 325°F, place the pies on the grill opposite hot coals. Cover and cook for 25–30 minutes, then rotate the pies a half turn for even cooking.

10 Cover the grill, cook for another 20–25 minutes. Check that the pies are done by inserting a toothpick (or similar) into the center of each pie—if it comes out clean, the pies are cooked. If not, continue cooking until the toothpick comes out clean.

11 Set the pies on rack to cool down.

12 Cut pies for serving and top with whipped cream.

13 Sit back, relax, and enjoy!

BBQ PIT BOYS
That smells
Guuuuuud...

■ SERVES: 6 | PREP TIME: 30 MINUTES | COOK TIME: 30 MINUTES ■

BLACKBERRY RHUBARB PIE

INGREDIENTS

- 4 cups blackberries
- 2 cups rhubarb, chopped
- ¾ cup white sugar, plus some for topping
- ½ cup all purpose flour
- 2 tbsp butter
- 2 packages pastry dough (or make your own)
- 1 egg
- ¼ cup milk

This wild blackberry rhubarb pie is cooked in a cast iron pan over charcoal, served with ice cream, is a real winner. Never let it be said you can't cook dessert on a BBQ grill.

METHOD

1 Mix the fruit ingredients with the flour and sugar.

2 Smear butter on the base and sides of a heavy pan or pie tray to prevent the pie from sticking. Lay the pastry into the base.

3 Mix the egg and milk and paint on to the pastry base. Place the fruit mix into the pie base.

4 Place the pastry lid on and pinch around the edges. Paint some egg wash on the top and sprinkle on some sugar to give a sweet crispy crust.

5 Place on a preheated grill around 375°F over indirect heat.

6 Cook for around 25–30 minutes until the pastry is done.

7 Serve hot or cold with ice cream or fresh cream.

CHOCOLATE BANANA DESSERT

INGREDIENTS

- 4–8 bananas
- 4–8 milk chocolate bars (or your favorite chocolate or caramel)

FOR SERVING

- vanilla ice cream
- crushed graham crackers
- caramel sauce

Kids of all ages love creamy melted chocolate stuffed bananas served warm off the grill. And it's a real easy to do side dish dessert!

METHOD

1 Bring grill temperature up to 300°F–350°F, with coals offset for indirect cooking.

2 Cut a slit along the length of each banana to make a pocket. Be sure not to cut all the way through.

3. Break chocolate into pieces and place in banana pocket.

4. Place bananas opposite hot coals for indirect cooking.

5. Cook for approximately one hour. Cook time may vary depending on temperature of your grill.

6. When ready, remove bananas from grill and place on a platter.

7. Top with graham crackers, caramel sauce, vanilla ice cream, and more chocolate.

8. Be sure to make enough for everyone. Sit back, relax, and enjoy!

GRANDMA'S GRILLED APPLE PIE

INGREDIENTS

- 8 baking apples
- 1 cup white sugar, plus some for the crust
- 1 tbsp flour
- ⅛ tsp salt
- 2 tsp lemon juice
- 2 premade pie dough sheets
- 1–2 tsp butter
- ¼ tsp cinnamon
- ⅛ tsp nutmeg

Fresh homemade apple pie served the way grandma would have—from her wood-fired kitchen stove—is as classic American food as it gets.

METHOD

1 Set up your grill for indirect grilling, with hot coals on one side of the grill and no coals on the other side. Preheat to a temperature of 425°F.

2 Core, peel, and slice the apples into ¼ to ⅜ inch slices, place in a bowl, and set aside.

3 In a second bowl, mix together the sugar, flour, and salt, then gradually add this mixture to the apples, stirring constantly to coat them well.

4 Add the lemon juice to the apples and stir to combine.

5 Unroll the premade dough and place it into the pie dish.

6 Spoon the apple mixture into the pie dish and sprinkle the nutmeg and cinnamon over the pie filling.

7 Place dots of butter on top of the filling, then cover with the second sheet of dough for the top pie crust.

8 Seal the pie crust edges together and score 4 slits in the top of the crust.

9 Sprinkle some sugar on top of the crust.

10 Place the pie on the side of the grill with no coals and cover the grill.

11 Cook time will be about 45 minutes. After 20 minutes, rotate the pie to promote even cooking.

12. After another 20–25 minutes, or when done, remove the pie from the grill, let the pie rest and cool down.

13 Slice the pie and serve with cheddar cheese, whipped cream, ice cream or your favorite accompaniment. Enjoy!

CHERRY CHOCOLATE PIE

INGREDIENTS

- 2 x 21 oz cans cherry pie filling
- 1 x 9-inch pie crust
- 1 roll pie dough for double crust top layer (optional)
- 1–2 chocolate candy bars

Check out our cherry chocolate pie dessert that's real quick and easy to make on the grill, as shown by the BBQ Pit Boys!

METHOD

1 Lay the pie crust into a pie dish.

2 Pour two cans of cherry pie filling into the pie crust.

3 Break up the chocolate into small pieces and add to the cherry filling.

4 Slice the roll of pie dough into strips. Carefully lay the strips across the pie in a lattice pattern.

5 Place pie in a covered grill at 400°F, away from the coals. After 15 minutes, turn the pie to cook evenly.

6 Cover the grill again, then lower the temperature to 350°F. Continue cooking for 30–45 minutes, or until the crust is browned the way you like it.

7 Cool or chill before serving.

Now I don't want any of you Pie Police telling me I don't know how to cut strips of pie dough. I'm just a BBQ Pit Boy, not Betty Crocker!

IRISH CREAM CHERRY PIE

INGREDIENTS

- 2 x 21 oz cans cherry pie filling
- 1 x 9-inch pie crust
- several oz Bailey's Irish Cream liquor
- 2 tbsp maple syrup

Check out our Bailey's Irish Cream cherry pie dessert that's real quick and easy to make!

METHOD

1 Preheat your grill to 400°F.

2 Lay the pie crust into a pie dish.

3 Pour two cans of cherry pie filling into the pie crust.

4 Add the Bailey's and maple syrup to the cherry filling.

5 Place on the grill over indirect heat and cover. Cook for 15 minutes, then turn the pie for an even bake.

6 Cover the grill again, reduce the temperature to 350°F, and cook for an additional 30–45 minutes.

7 Allow the pie to cool before slicing, then serve with a scoop of vanilla ice cream.

GRILLED BACON BOURBON CRÈME BRÛLÉE

INGREDIENTS

- 2 cups cream
- 2 tsp vanilla extract
- 2 tbsp brown sugar
- 6 egg yolks
- 8 slices of bacon, fried and chopped finely
- 1½ cups bourbon

Check out our recipe for a kicked-up version of a classic dessert, grilled bacon bourbon crème brûlée!

METHOD

1 Preheat the grill to 300°F, set up for indirect cooking.

2 Pour the cream into a medium size pan over indirect heat on the grill. Stirring all the time, add the vanilla extract followed by the sugar and the egg yolks. Stir until well combined and smooth.

3 Pour the cream mixture into four individual oven-to-table shallow dishes and place them on a baking sheet on the grill. Cover and cook about 30 minutes until the mixture is set.

4 Remove from the grill, pour the bourbon equally over the top of each dessert. Refrigerate for at least an hour.

5 Immediately before serving, sprinkle some sugar over the top of each dessert and caramelize using a small blow torch. Alternatively, you can use the broiler in your kitchen.

6 Serve with crumbled bacon pieces on top. Enjoy!

BACON OREO BBQ COOKIES

INGREDIENTS

- 1 package Oreo cookies, Mega Stuf
- 1–2 packages bacon slices, regular cut
- barbeque sauce, your favorite

PITMASTER TIP

Make sure you use regular cut bacon not thick cut, as thick will take too long to cook.

This recipe is perfect to do while you're sharing a beer—the cook time is just about as long as you need for a beer!

METHOD

1 Set up the grill with coals offset for indirect cooking.

2 Wrap each cookie with a slice of bacon and place on the grill over indirect heat. Cover and cook until the bacon is as crispy as you like it.

3 Baste the bacon covered cookies with your favorite barbeque sauce. Cook for about another 10–15 minutes.

4 Let them cool down completely before eating. Enjoy!

CREDITS AND ACKNOWLEDGMENTS

PUBLISHER'S ACKNOWLEDGMENTS

*All photographs are courtesy of the BBQ Pit Boys, Alamy, or Shutterstock.
For information on any photographs other than sourced from bbqpitboys.com,
please contact: info@moseleyroad.com*

Now go 'n' get grillin'!

*"To the BBQ Pit Boys, masters of the grill and guardians of the flame. Your passion for barbecue
inspires countless enthusiasts worldwide to explore the art of outdoor cooking. With every
sizzle and smoke, you bring people together to share ideas, help teach a new generation how to
provide for themselves, families and others, and to turn simple meals into memorable feasts.
Your dedication to traditional techniques and innovative recipes reminds us that barbecue is
more than just a way of cooking; it's a way of life. Here's to many more years of great food, good
friends, and the shared joy of barbecue Thumbs-Up and BPB4L!"*

Bobby Fame